EPSON

Complete Guide to
Digital Printing

EPSON Complete Guide to Digital Printing, Revised and Updated Edition

Book design and layout: Sandy Knight
Cover design: Sandy Knight
Cover photo of girl: ©Robert Ganz
Cover photo of pink flower: ©Joseph R. Meehan
Product photographs provided courtesy of the manufacturers
Editorial assistance: Mimi Netzel and Delores Gosnell

Library of Congress Cataloging-in-Publication Data

Sheppard, Rob.
  Epson complete guide to digital printing / Rob Sheppard.-- Rev. & updated ed.
    p. cm.
  Includes index.
  ISBN 1-57990-705-9 (pbk.)
  1. Epson printers. 2. Digital printing. 3. Image processing--Digital
techniques. 4. Images, Photographic--Data processing. I. Epson (Firm) II.
Title. III. Title: Complete guide to digital printing.
  TK7887.7.S48 2005
  686.2'3--dc22

                             2005000406

10 9 8 7 6 5 4 3 2 1

Revised and Updated Edition

Published by Lark Books, a division of
Sterling Publishing Co., Inc.
387 Park Avenue South, New York, N.Y. 10016

© 2005, Rob Sheppard
Photography © 2005, Rob Sheppard unless otherwise specified

Distributed in Canada by Sterling Publishing,
c/o Canadian Manda Group, 165 Dufferin Street
Toronto, Ontario, Canada M6K 3H6

Distributed in the U.K. by Guild of Master Craftsman Publications Ltd., Castle Place,
166 High Street, Lewes, East Sussex, England BN7 1XU
Tel: (+ 44) 1273 477374, Fax: (+ 44) 1273 478606
Email: pubs@thegmcgroup.com, Web: www.gmcpublications.com

Distributed in Australia by Capricorn Link (Australia) Pty Ltd.,
P.O. Box 704, Windsor, NSW 2756 Australia

If you have questions or comments about this book, please contact:
Lark Books
67 Broadway
Asheville, NC 28801
(828) 253-0467

Manufactured in China

ISBN: 1-57990-705-9

For information about custom editions, special sales, premium and corporate purchases, please contact Sterling Special
Sales Department at 800-805-5489 or specialsales@sterlingpub.com.

Complete Guide to
Digital Printing
Revised and Updated

ROB SHEPPARD

LARK BOOKS

A Division of Sterling Publishing Co., Inc.
New York

Contents

Introduction

Prints have long been the ideal expression of a photographic image. You can hold a print, display it proudly on the wall, offer it for sale — in other words share your photos with others in a very tangible way. There are new ways of viewing images, from sending them between cell phones to putting them up on a website, but none seem as substantial as a print.

This book is for photographers. It is not designed to make you a technical expert, just to encourage and support your efforts in getting a better print from your digital image files. I am more interested in helping you make a good print than making you conversant in computer speak. I am excited about the possibilities of digital photography, and ink jet prints are an expression of those possibilities.

Making a satisfying print is about having fun and enjoying photography, whether for pleasure or profit. I can assure you that everything in this book will work for the average photographer. I have checked all the techniques described here myself, plus taught much of it at workshops and seminars. You don't need to be a technical genius to use the information. This book is about making digital photography fun for everyone.

I genuinely believe that making beautiful pictures is fun and exciting. Sometimes people see my photos and tell me they wished they could get such "good prints." You can do it, too! This book will show you how.

To be fair, I really have to put in a warning: making great prints can be hazardous to your sleep. I hear this again and again. You get going on tweaking that little extra bit of detail out of the print, and you get so engrossed that time passes quickly. Past bedtime!

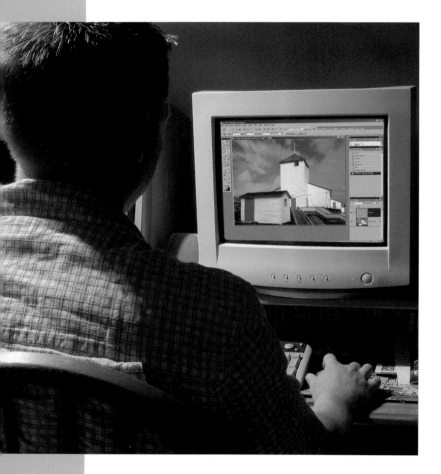

This book is written from the perspective of a photographer. Engineers, computer enthusiasts, and other non-photographers have written a lot of the information that is available about computers and photography. The technology is very important, but an overemphasis on it can obscure the main reason

most of us are working with the computer—better photographs, better prints.

I admit my bias. I don't really care about slavishly following all the technical rules. I do care about photos ... and prints. This is a craft, every bit as much as printmakers practice in the darkroom. The digital print has been key in a resurgence of interest in photography. We now have so much more control over our images. While much is done on the computer with Adobe Photoshop and other image-processing software, the print is the most satisfying part of the experience.

In spite of the number of books that are available for photographers working on an image in the computer, very little is out there on making a great print. Sure, there is some discussion of printing, but too often it is limited to talking about color management as if that were all there is to printing. Great prints can be both more and less than strict color management.

Sure, we'll talk a bit about color management. But if this is something you've avoided, because it seems too technical, here's a subversive thought that you'll want to keep in mind: you can get great prints without being overwhelmed by color management.

We'll talk more about all of these things as we go through the book. I'm going to give you lots of ideas —you pick what works best for you in your situation and for your prints. A great print, again, is one that satisfies you, no matter what anyone else says.

Now you might wonder who I am. I have long been a photographer—I made my first darkroom when I was thirteen (now I have kids that age and older!). I worked on my high-school yearbook, then the college newspaper, and started to sell my first photos while still in school. I've worked as a photojournalist, nature photographer, videographer, film and video producer, photography teacher, and how-to writer. I am the second editor of *Outdoor Photographer* magazine, and the first editor (and co-developer) of *PCPhoto* magazine.

How this Book Can Be Used

This book is a collection of lots of information on making better prints—just like a workshop. You can go through it bit by bit, working out your own procedures based on what is in the book, if that works for you. Read it straight through if you'd like (there is a logical progression in topics) or just keep it as a reference as needed. Skip around to the most interesting parts for you. Or if you want to impress your friends and family that you really have studied ink jet printing, use it to decorate your desk.

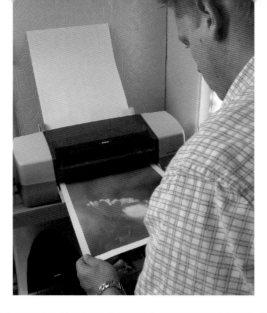

Here's an overview of how the book and its chapters are put together so you can best use it to help you with your specific printing needs:

1 **Jumpstart Into Printing—** A quick overview of the key steps and concerns you need to know in order to get started making great photographic prints from your printer.

2 **Selecting a Printer—** What features can be found on a printer? How do they affect performance and price?

3 **Starting with the Right Paper—** The paper you choose is critical to making a great print. Here's how to choose the best paper for your project.

4 **Getting Technical—** Technical issues that affect digital imaging and how images play out as a print are explained, including the always-challenging issue of resolution.

5 **Refining the Image for Printing—**Image-processing Programs—A good image-processing program allows you to make better prints by adjusting the image in many ways. Some tips on selecting the right program are included.

6 **Refining the Image for Printing—** Tonal Adjustments—The brightness and contrast of a photo strongly affect the appearance of the print. Learn the key tools to adjust both.

7 **Refining the Image for Printing—** Color Adjustments—Color used to be considered "unchangeable" in a print, but that's not true today! You'll see how color can be enhanced and adjusted for your printing needs.

8 **Finishing Touches—** Try these to turn a good print into a great print, from sharpening to borders.

9 **Dialing in the Print—** The perennial challenge, how can you make that print look more like what you see on the monitor? What's color management all about and do you really need it?

10 **Displaying the Print—** Photo, photo on the wall, where's the best place to put them all?

11 **Printing Projects—** There are many things you can do with your photos besides making great display prints.

12 **Black-and-White and Panoramic Prints—** Use these tips to make better black-and-white prints from your ink jet and discover the advantages of using a color image for better black-and-whites! And, the big, wide print—how do you shoot for it and print it out?

13 **Making Long-Lived Prints—** Nowadays, you can count on your printer to deliver long-lasting prints, although this wasn't always true. Epson's ink jet printers easily deliver prints that will last as long as a traditional color print, and some of the newest Epson technologies can beat that by far.

14 **Taking Care of Your Printer—**While Epson printers are generally trouble-free, they do need some care. Here are some tips to let you get the most from your printer by taking good care of it.

Jumpstart into Printing

Let's get into printing quickly. I want you to have a quick guide to making prints so you can discover the joy and excitement right away. If you follow the steps in this chapter, you'll be able to get pleasing prints immediately. We've got the rest of the book to go into details on printers and refining your print. In addition, this guide will give you an overview of the printing process that you can refer back to at any time as you read the rest of the book.

Finding an Image

You might have thought we'd start with the printer. A printer is obviously very important to the process, but you have to have an image to print first. A challenge faced by too many photographers is finding the photo on the computer's hard drive (or other media). You may have scanned a slide or negative, gotten a CD of images from your processor, or downloaded photos from your digital camera— all great ways to get an image into the computer.

But then you have to find the right photo in order to print it! I know from experience that this can be frustrating. Where did it go? Which folder is it in? And then which picture file is the right one?

You have several excellent options here. I always recommend that people use some sort of image browser program. This software allows you a visual look at the photos on your hard drive, so you actually see images rather than just file names. It makes it so much easier to find photos.

Windows XP has a simple, integrated image browser built into the operating system. When you open a folder, the photos show up as little "thumbnails" (small images). Among a number of options, you can set up a folder to see one photo and a "filmstrip" of smaller images (a few at a time) or all of your images at once as same-size thumbnails. While the photos aren't big, you can get a good idea of which image you want. You can even print from this point or launch the image directly into a photo program.

Many Epson printers include a more advanced browser and printing program called Film Factory. This easy-to-use software allows you to quickly review images on your hard drive (as well as download them directly from a digital camera) as moderate-sized thumbnails. You can rename photos, set up new folders, group photos into categories (called "Film Cases") and do some simple processing on them fast and easy. The program includes many excellent options for printing, including multiple photos on a page and album pages. This program is available for both Mac and Windows.

A step up in capability can be found in image management programs like ACD Systems ACDSee (www.acdsystems.com), iView Media and Media Pro (www.iview-multimedia.com), Jasc AfterShot (www.jasc.com), and Adobe Photoshop Album (www.adobe.com). These offer much more flexibility in viewing, sorting, and editing your photographs directly from a drive. They also include the ability to create albums and attach keywords so you can find your images more easily.

Finding and organizing your images on your computer hard drive is the first step to successful printing.

Windows XP includes a simple image browser that shows a thumbnail of each file.

Film Factory, a browser and printer program from Epson, allows you to see and organize images.

iView Media Pro is typical of browser programs that allow you to see and organize thumbnails, as well as print an index of images from many files (at right).

These four browser programs offer one feature that facilitates making prints: index prints. These are also called proof sheets or "contact" prints (named after traditional darkroom techniques—Windows XP also allows a limited contact sheet to be made). These printouts give you multiple choices in how you make a print of all the photo files from a file folder or disk by providing a hardcopy visual index.

I think this is huge! Now you can find the photo you want by quickly skimming through a few printed pages to find the exact image and name. You don't have to open multiple folders on your computer or put a lot of disks in and out of the machine. The index print shows you what you want from your hard drive, a CD, or any other place you have images stored and it is viewable anytime, anywhere. I file my index prints with my CD's—that makes them so much more usable.

You want to make a print of that great sunset over the Pacific, or maybe the shot of the kids at the soccer tournament? Check those index prints, find the file and the location, open it and start printing!

How to Make Stunning Prints from the Start

Of course, to make a great print, you need a capable printer. All Epson printers on the market today make superb photo-quality prints, as good, or even better than what you might get from your local minilab. However, how you use that printer is really critical if you want to get the most from it. Let's look at some of the key steps to making photo prints that you can be proud of:

1 **Open the photo file**

You can open your photo with a special printing program or image-processing software. Make any adjustments you think you will need to correct and enhance the subject.

◀ One key element in making a great print is to use the appropriate file size and dpi/ppi.

2 **Use the appropriate file size**

Your image-processing program will give you a file size. This is so important. Again and again, I have seen good images become poor prints because there was not enough data to support the print size. Without that needed information, print quality will fall off, affecting sharpness, color, tonalities, and more.

The tricky thing, though, is that printers are so good today that they can make almost any print look acceptable in overall color and sharpness, even if there isn't adequate picture data. This can easily fool the viewer into thinking this is the best they can get, when it really isn't. Depending on the printer and paper, expect a 4 x 6 inch photo to print best with a 4–5 MB file (uncompressed TIFF size), a 5 x 7 with a 7–10 MB file, and an 8 x 10 with a 14–20 MB file.

3 **Use the right image file dpi/ppi**

This one causes all sorts of confusion. The important thing to remember is that the image file will have a dots-per-inch/pixels-per-inch size (dpi/ppi). This is not the same as the printer's dpi. Each refers to different things in the process.

Your image should be at 200–300 dpi/ppi and sized to the print dimensions. (Proper image size is critical because resolution is referenced to this size). You may hear higher resolutions recommended, but I've ever found anyone that can see an appreciable difference at standard print sizes. Epson printer algorithms do a superb job with this range of resolution. If you go much lower, or figure that more is better and go a lot higher, you will find that print quality deteriorates.

► While paper choice is a matter of personal taste, the intended use of the print should also be considered.

4 **Choose the right paper**

You've probably heard the realtor's mantra of "location, location, and location." Consider "paper, paper, and paper" to be as important in making a good print. This is so important that I expand on paper choices in the next few steps. You are always safe with Epson's papers—you have both quality and creative options with them. You can also test other papers that have unusual surfaces not offered by Epson.

5 **Check your paper's weight and usage**

The weight of a paper is very important. You need to be sure that it is heavy enough for its intended use. Some of the sharpest, most beautiful prints come from thin, plastic papers. However, these can be uncomfortable to hold and share, if that is important (because they seem very flimsy even though they are quite sturdy). The weight of a photo has less effect when the image is framed and put on display. But if you need a brochure to circulate, you had better be sure the paper is heavy enough to withstand it.

6 **Confirm your paper's whiteness value**

A white paper gives you pure colors and brighter overall tones in the print. Most papers have a whiteness rating, so check this value (in the 90s is good). Whiteness may not be as critical with some specialty papers (such as certain watercolor papers used for photo printing), because their special tonality is part of the desired effect.

7 **Selecting the paper surface**

For the best color, sharpness, and tonal range, use a glossy paper. However, this is not a surface that everyone likes. Gloss means shine, and shiny surfaces can be too reflective of bright things around you, making the image harder to see. Matte papers do offer excellent color, sharpness, and tonal range, and many photographers prefer their look. Luster surfaces are in-between. Try making some tests in your own computer system to find your preference.

You can also choose among many specialty papers, including canvas, silk, transparency, watercolor, and more for specific and unique printing effects.

8 Setting the printer driver

I have been surprised more than once by advanced photographers and even pros that don't know that there is a printer driver. This is a dedicated software program that controls how the printer works with an image. The driver's default settings, however, are rarely optimum for photos.

The printer driver is loaded when you tell your computer to print. You'll get a dialogue box that will likely be very simple. To access advanced driver controls, you have to select Properties in the printer dialogue box. In Mac, many driver settings will come up with the print dialogue box. Most drivers will ask you for a paper choice, a quality/speed mode, orientation, and color adjustments.

Usually when you choose a paper, the driver automatically chooses the best print quality/ speed for it. Orientation will be Portrait (vertical) or Landscape (horizontal). If you have color management controls (such as ICM), try them at this point. Other settings like Epson's PhotoEnhance can be quite useful (it automatically makes some adjustments to the photo to enhance details and color).

9 Making a test

For anyone who has worked in a darkroom, testing is second nature. We always used to make a test print, then check it for exposure, dodging, and burning, and so on. Unfortunately, the hype of numerous people in the computer industry has convinced many photographers that the key to a good print is ... more equipment! Better prints are just a short step away, and you don't always need more equipment.

I've often said that printing really is a craft, in part because it is so subjective. A good print for one person may not please someone else. The craft of printing is mastered by making a lot of prints, testing different papers, settings, etc., then using those tests to refine the image.

▲ **The printer driver tells the printer how to make the best print on a particular paper.**

In addition, no matter how good your monitor is and how well it is matched to your printing, a print is not the same as a monitor-based image. It is best to evaluate your photos as prints—do they meet your expectations or not? They do not need to fit someone else's arbitrary standards that may have nothing to do with your situation—they should meet your specific needs.

10 Recording Adjustments

After you make a test, you should have a better idea of what adjustments are needed for a typical good print (brighter or darker settings than what looks good on the screen, different color adjustments, and so on). Write those down! As long as you use the same printer and paper, these basic adjustments should not change. With most Epson printers, you can also save these settings with the printer driver— we'll explain that later.

Selecting a Printer

Ink jet printers have come a long way from the first models. They were slow, of poor quality, black-and-white only, and could produce nothing that looked like a photograph. Today, ink jet printers offer color, superb text, and photo-quality.

If you are in the market for an ink jet, whether it is a new purchase or an upgrade, you will find a great range of printers on the market. There are definitely differences, so let's look at the ink jet printer to give you a better idea of what makes them different. Then you can decide what makes a difference to you.

How Ink Jet Printers Create Quality Photo Prints

With an ink jet printer, ink is sprayed in tiny droplets onto the paper in a distinct pattern to make all the tones and colors you expect in a photograph. Some folks have given this a French name, giclee (shee-CLAY) printing (which just means sprayed ink prints) to make it seem like some exotic, European technology (so they can charge more for the prints, I think).

Epson printers lay down the ink with a patented piezo-electric printing head. There are variants of this head depending on the level of printer, the number of inks, etc., but basically, this head translates the electrical impulses that represent your photo into drops of ink that are rapidly placed onto your paper to create a beautiful photograph.

Micro piezo technology results in very consistent and precise ink droplets, allowing the printer head to place them extremely accurately, yet at high speed. The printing head actually changes position as it puts these droplets down, running back and forth across the paper as the printer moves the paper in small steps under it. And still with extraordinary precision!

Piezo Element
Vibration Plate
Ink Droplet
Communication Hole
Nozzle
Ink Chamber
Ink Supply Hole
Ink Reservoir

▲ **Epson's patented piezo-electric printing head precisely places tiny drops of ink on the paper to form a photo-quality image.**

This builds the photo, row by row, inch by inch. Thousands of tiny drops of ink are put down very quickly when you consider they all have to line up exactly right in order to make a photo-quality print. Epson has included a special feature in the printer driver (or software) called AcuPhoto halftoning, which produces accurate color with true photo gradations. In fact, Epson has some amazing, proprietary algorithms (computer instructions in the program) which optimize the image in the print. Top photo quality is highly dependent on a printer's ability to lay down ink in exact patterns and alignments.

▲ **In the picture on the right, smaller ink droplets (shown greatly magnified so the droplets are visible) give better tonal gradations and color rendition than the coarser droplets on the left.**

In addition, the resolution of the printer (such as 1440 x 720 or 2880 x 1440 dpi) affects how the ink is applied. While higher resolution (up to a point) can produce more detail in shadows and highlights (two of the toughest areas for a printer to deal with), as well as crisper text and fine lines, top photo-quality is not dependent on the highest printer resolution.

Epson printers use ink dots so small that you cannot see them with the naked eye. With smaller droplets, print quality gets better because the printed dots can be blended better and gradations of tone are smoother. This can be more important than resolution.

The droplets themselves come in four distinct colors: cyan, magenta, yellow, and black. All Epson printers have these four colors. The six-color, or photo printers, add pale versions of cyan and magenta to improve color tonalities. This technique is especially noticeable in the highlights and in subtle gradations between tones. The seven-color printers add light gray to the mix for better neutral tones and for increased ability to render subtle tonal gradations. Some manufacturers build black from cyan, magenta, and yellow and reserve the black ink for text, while others make black in a photo from the combination of colors. Epson uses all of the ink

colors, including black, in photos to gain better shadow detail, purer blacks, and a denser black that makes the overall photo have more brilliance than even a traditional print from your minilab.

Finally, ink comes out wet, of course, so Epson has engineered a printing process with their ink formulation and printing head so that the ink dries very rapidly. This keeps prints from smearing and makes them water-resistant.

Dyes vs. Pigments

Ink jet printers use two basic types of inks: dyes or pigments. Dyes have traditionally offered brighter colors, but are more likely to fade than pigments. For a long time dyes were the only way to print with an ink jet, since they were the only way to get colored ink through the printing head. It was difficult to develop pigments that didn't clog the head.

Epson was the first to beat both problems. They developed a dye-based ink with improved fade resistance. They also figured out how to make pigmented ink that both flowed easily through the print head and produced bright, saturated colors. Although dyes hold a slight edge for color brilliance and speed of printing, that probably won't last long given Epson engineering ingenuity.

What to Consider When Buying a Printer

Epson makes a whole range of printers from inexpensive all-purpose home printers to specialized photo printers to large graphic arts printers. Different models have different features. Here are some key features to consider when comparing printers:

1 Number of colors

Generally, you will pay for more colors in a printer. Low-priced units typically come with four colors: cyan, magenta, yellow, and black. Epson's algorithms get a lot out of those four colors, so you really can get photo-quality images from them. For really fine prints, you need the six- to eight-color printers. The extra inks allow for much finer gradations of color and tone. Prints look richer with better tonalities. Dark and light tones are especially enhanced.

2 Droplet size

While there is a lot of hype about resolution in the printer market, a far more important part of the technology is ink droplet size. As droplets decrease in size, tonal gradations are improved, colors are more accurate, and the print has more detail in the highlights and shadows. Epson printers have some of the smallest droplet sizes on the market.

3 Resolution

I wish this could be explained simply and concisely—it is very important and confusing at the same time. There is a section in this book that covers resolution in greater detail. For now, just keep this in mind—printer resolution is not the same as image resolution. Image resolution is how pixels are arranged in a photo; printer resolution is how ink is applied to the paper. Current Epson printers are at least 1440 x 720 dpi, which is enough for nearly all photographic purposes. Higher resolutions can slow down printing and provide little or no increase in print quality. If you are not sure of this, try it. I think you will not see a difference.

4 Speed

Printers get faster all the time and price generally increases with speed. In looking at the speed of a printer, however, you need to know several things. First, print speed is limited by the computer's processing speed and available RAM—it takes some computing power to process a file for printing and photos are especially greedy. Second, the industry has no absolute standard of speed so you cannot compare brands, just printers within a brand. Third, the industry has some funny conventions about the way speeds are marketed.

Typically, the advertised fast speeds are for draft or economy mode, which you are unlikely to use with photos. No printer can produce a photo at speeds of 10 pages of color per minute. Photos can take minutes and still be fast. Compare fine, best, or photo-quality printing speeds. Epson always includes information on photo-printing speeds with its dedicated photo printers.

5 Borderless capabilities

Borderless prints have become standard in the ink jet industry. The photo comes out of the printer with no white borders and no trimming needed. Most of Epson's photo printers offer this option. However, borderless printing may only be possible with specific print sizes.

6 Paper path

If you want to print on very thick papers (up to 1.5mm), check into some of the higher-end Epson printers that include multiple paper paths. You need a straight-through paper path that allows the printer to print on the paper without needing to bend it.

7 Size

Big printers cost more, no question about that. The least expensive printers will handle standard 8 ½ x 11 paper just fine, but no bigger. The midrange Epson printers (and up) can produce panoramics at 8 ½ x 44 inches. Larger printers typically handle standard print sizes up to 13 x 19 plus panoramics to 13 x 44 inches. The really big roll printers start at 24 inches wide and go up from there.

▲ **A printer with borderless printing capability will print to the edge of the paper so that no trimming is necessary.**

8 Grouped or individual ink cartridges

Ink typically comes in black plus a color cartridge or in individual packages for each color. Lower-priced printers usually have the grouped color cartridge. Individual cartridges can be more efficient if you do a lot of printing because you can replace each color as you deplete it.

9 CD printing

Epson pioneered the capability to print directly onto specially made CDs. If you like burning your own CDs, this can be a great feature. It allows you to personalize your CDs without messy or hard-to-use, stick-on labels. You can print text, photos, and special designs. CD slide shows are becoming increasingly popular, and CD printing just makes them look great.

10 Accessories

You may have some specific needs, such as printing long panoramics or doing prints on a roll (convenient for printing lots of 4 x 6-inch photos, for example). Check to see if the printer you are considering can use these accessories.

11 Pro-printers vs. consumer types

Pro printers cost quite a bit more than consumer models, yet on the surface, they often seem to have similar features. Underneath the hood, so to speak, they do offer some things that can be very important to professionals who make a lot of prints. Pro-printers are designed for steady, dependable use under the pressure of making nonstop prints, day after day. In addition, their tolerances are so tight that a print done one day looks pretty much identical to the same image printed another day. Some pro models use large ink tanks to make ink usage more efficient for the heavy user.

12 Print life

Pigment-based inks have more potential for long life than dye-based inks, and Epson has pioneered the use of pigment inks for printers at every price point. Their pigment-based Durabrite inks for general-purpose printers are water, smudge, and light resistant. The UltraChrome pigment-based inks used in the photo printers do all that, plus add richer color and even longer life.

13 Connectivity

There are two basic types of computer-to-printer connections: USB and FireWire. USB comes in two types, the older USB 1.0 and the much faster USB 2.0. To gain the full benefits of USB 2.0, you must have a USB 2.0 port on the computer. USB 2.0 and FireWire both offer faster data transfer when connecting any peripheral to a computer.

Epson printers do offer networking capabilities, and a few units have been introduced with optional Bluetooth wireless capabilities so that a cable connection is not required between the computer and printer.

14 All-in-one printers

All-in-one printers incorporate a flatbed scanner in them and minimize the use of desktop space. They can be used to scan photos to the computer or to scan images and print them directly. Various features include the ability to scan prints, slides, and negatives, the potential to print directly from a digital camera's memory card, and even fax capability (on the SOHO models). Epson also includes remarkable, "one-touch" software with some of these units for fixing old photos.

16 Direct printing

Direct printing has become an important option for the digital photographer. You can print directly with enabled Epson printers in two ways:

1. Pictbridge—when you use a PictBridge compatible camera, you can connect the camera directly to the printer for printing.

2. Memory cards—you can remove your card from the camera, plug it into the appropriate slot on the printer, and start printing.

© Bruce Dale

Bruce Dale

National Geographic and Beyond

Bruce Dale has produced over 2,000 published photographs for *National Geographic,* and is also a well-established advertising photographer. He teaches photography and the use of digital technologies, and is a frequent lecturer.

One of the very early adopters of Epson printers for photography, his first printer was actually one of the first models of dot matrix printers that Epson introduced around 1980. He used some of the earliest Stylus Photo printers to begin making color prints from digital files back in the mid-1990s.

Today he uses a smaller Stylus Photo ink jet for traveling and keeps it stowed in his truck. In his office, he has three more Epson printers: a high-volume model that gives him fast and reliable general prints, a larger desktop unit for brilliant and accurate aim prints, and a wide-format printer for gallery prints.

Dale says that the biggest impact of Epson printers on his business is in the final quality of the image. For example, he can make a small proof print that translates identically to a large mural size image. Before, with conventional color printing, he always had to factor in such things as color shifts and reciprocity changes due to printing time. Now, he feels he has total control over the finished product from text to portfolio prints and gallery prints. Furthermore, he always includes aim prints with all digital files sent out for publication, to let the recipients know what the final image should look like. And he incorporates Epson printers in his workshop classes as a teaching tool.

His favorite papers for the desktop printers are Epson's Premium Luster papers, and he uses Epson's Premium Glossy for aim prints. For the big gallery prints, most of his printing is on Epson's Premium Luster paper. For him, choosing the right media is extremely important. He believes Epson has done a great job of fine-tuning their inks and papers to give optimum results.

Dale believes that digital photography and printing have literally surged into serious use much faster than anyone expected. Many printing obstacles and barriers of the past (inferior paper, slow speeds, poor longevity) have fallen by the wayside. But that doesn't mean he isn't looking forward to what's coming next.

Dale's Web site is www.brucedale.com.

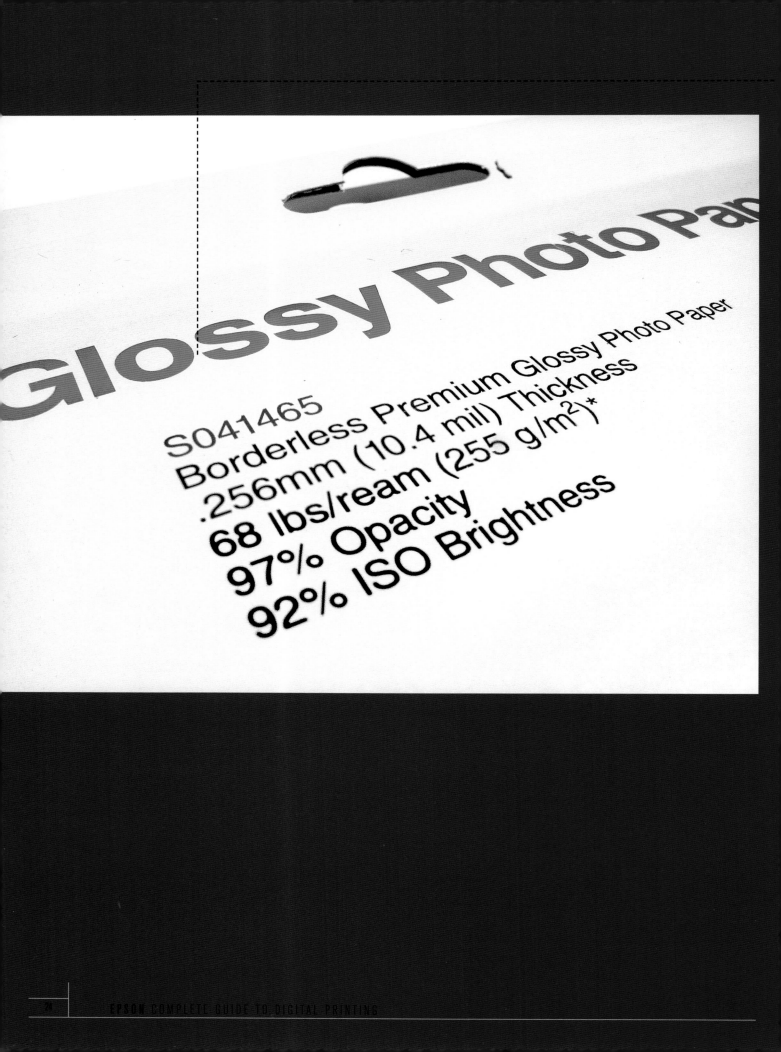

Glossy Photo Paper

S041465
Borderless Premium Glossy Photo Paper
.256mm (10.4 mil) Thickness
68 lbs/ream (255 g/m²)*
97% Opacity
92% ISO Brightness

Starting with the Right Paper

Ink jet printers have almost improved too much for their own good. They impress marketing types so much that the equipment is often promoted as being capable of superb results on any paper. While it is true that ink jet printers can make prints on cheap paper look halfway decent, they really need quality paper designed for photos in order to produce the best photo prints.

Epson alone makes a wide variety of papers, and there is a growing marketplace of ink jet papers from many suppliers. This large selection of papers can be confusing, but it is also a wonderful thing for photographers, because we can choose exactly the right paper best suited to meet our needs.

There are a number of factors that go into choosing that right paper. In the end, this is a highly personal choice (for example, I may love matte papers, but you think glossy is the only way to go). As you gain experience with the many choices, you will be able to make prints that are a real joy to produce.

However, while lots of papers are "available," you might not be able to find them at a given store.

Check office supply and photo stores as well as the Web. You can buy all Epson papers off the Web if needed. Don't be over influenced by well-meaning but uninformed sales people at retail locations. I have actually had the experience of someone at an office supply store telling me a paper had been discontinued—this would have been a big surprise to the manufacturer. They just didn't have the paper and didn't really understand the paper market.

Paper Weight and Thickness

Every paper has a weight and a thickness. These are both "technical" terms of sorts and a subjective impression you have of a paper. They affect how a paper can be used as well as an impression you get while viewing the photograph—really! A paper's weight and thickness have a psychological impact, which we'll cover in a minute.

All papers can be given a specific weight in pounds (per ream, based on an industry convention for paper dimensions). Thicker papers will usually weigh more, so the weight will give you an idea of how a paper will feel. You may run across a few papers that are full of air, so they can be lighter although still thick. In this case, you have to look at the paper's thickness rating. Paper is also often described in weight terminology, such as a heavyweight paper.

► **Paper weight is important in determining the best choice for a project. In general, heavier papers also convey an impression of quality.**

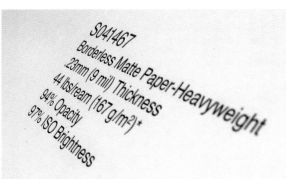

S041467
Borderless Matte Paper-Heavyweight
.23mm (9 mil) Thickness
44 lbs/ream (167 g/m²)*
94% Opacity
97% ISO Brightness

▲ **The surface of photo-quality paper can range from glossy to matte. This is a subjective choice that affects the appearance of the finished print.**

The bottom line for the photographer is what do you expect from your print? You need a heavier weight paper if the print will be handled a lot, such as passing around to friends and family. Brochures or flyers, too, need some weight or they'll leave a poor impression with recipients. If the print is going to be mounted behind glass, weight is less important.

Opacity

Opacity might be better understood if you think of it in terms of transparency. How easily can you see through the paper? If not very well, the paper has a high opacity. If you can easily see through the paper, it has a low opacity. The thickness and weight of a paper have a strong effect on its opacity. It is measured in a percentage with 0% being fully transparent (no opacity) and 100% fully opaque.

This becomes important when you need to put papers together (as in a booklet) or if you need to print on both sides (such as a brochure). With low opacity, you can see words or photos coming through. High opacity makes the photo stand out on the page, regardless of what is below it. Look for high opacity papers when you do business printing, such as brochures and newsletters.

Surface

The surface of ink jet paper is generally coated or prepared to accept the ink and give the best prints. Printing photographs on inexpensive, uncoated paper can cause the ink to run and "bleed," resulting in blurry, unsatisfactory prints.

The available surface textures of ink jet papers run from glossy (very shiny) to matte (non-reflective) with variations such as semigloss and luster in-between. Choosing the right surface is highly subjective. Many photographers like glossy paper because images look very sharp, colors appear brilliant, and the prints look like traditional glossy photographs. However, not everyone likes a reflective surface for every subject. Matte- or luster-finish papers are often preferred for photos of people. High-quality papers will give excellent color, sharpness, and brilliance in any surface finish. Papers like Epson Watercolor Radiant White have a matte finish and produce rich tonalities that give prints a "fine-art" quality.

Your end use also can affect your paper choice. Glossy papers do not fold well, so if you need to make a brochure or a greeting card, either use a matte paper or buy specially-made papers that are scored to fold easily. In addition, glossy papers, in general, have a shorter life than matte papers, but this varies depending on the inks used, the specific paper, and print storage. (More on paper and print life on the next page and in Chapter 13.)

Whiteness

Papers do get rated for whiteness (or ISO brightness). Higher numbers mean whiter papers. Typically, you want as white a paper as possible (rated in the 90s or higher) because that means your colors will be their brightest and the tonalities their richest. However, when using specialty products such as watercolor paper, where a warm tone is part of the appeal, a reduced whiteness value may be desirable.

Life

All paper ages. It may yellow and deteriorate from exposure to light and certain gases in the air (including pollution). Cheap paper may have acids in it that can degrade the paper itself (and therefore the image) after a few years. Better papers vary from acid-free to plastic coated to minimize this problem.

The inks that are used also limit a photo's life. Dye-based inks do not last as long as pigments. However, any ink will last longer with the right paper. Some Epson papers are specifically designed to work with the ink to increase its life. For archival pigments, there are matching archival papers that make a very long-lasting combination. While you can mix papers designed for dye-based and pigment based inks with the other ink type for effect, this is really not a good idea, as the dye-based inks really do interact differently with paper than pigments.

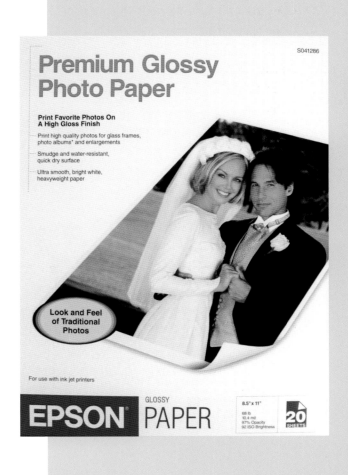

Use

How you plan to use your prints affects paper choice. Will people be handling your prints? You should use a heavier paper. Do you plan to make brochures? Be sure the paper folds properly. Do you need to print on both sides? Be sure your paper is coated for two-sided printing. Do you want to sell prints? Consider the feel, look, and longevity of the image on the paper.

Ink Type

Epson printers use either pigment-based or dye-based inks. It is very important to know what ink type your printer uses and choose a paper accordingly. While some papers will handle all ink types, most do not. Pigment-based inks do not work well on papers designed for dye-based inks. Dye-based inks will not look their best on papers made for pigment-based inks.

Specialty Papers

Specialty papers and printing media may offer specific solutions to your photo needs that regular papers can't provide. You may want to explore the specialty papers that are available and discover what they can do for your photography. One area that can provide some really beautiful results are the watercolor and fine-art papers. These papers add a certain richness and depth to the image. Epson's fine-art papers are 100% cotton-fiber, acid-free paper available in several surface textures.

You can find also find specialty printing media that allow you to use your images in very unique ways. These include iron-on transfer paper to put a photo on a T-shirt, photo stickers, scrapbooking media, and more. Some of the really specialized "papers", such as metallic, silk, and transparency material can be hard to find except on the Web. If you want to experiment, the range of printable paper possibilities can enhance your photos.

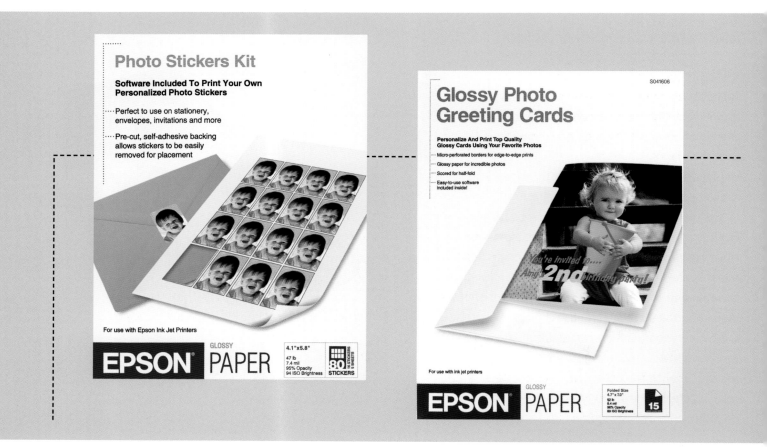

Rolls and Sheets

Rolls and large sheets of paper are important for printers that can handle them. A number of Epson printers offer roll-paper handling capabilities, which make it easy to print multiple prints without having to deal with single sheets of paper, as well as create long panoramic images. A number of Epson printers even include an automatic print cutter that will allow you to leave your printer unattended while it prints and cuts your photos.

With borderless printing and paper rolls, it is quite easy to produce multiple 4 x 6 prints like those you get at the mini-lab, except that the printing is under your control. The printer pulls the roll paper in as needed and you get a long strip of borderless prints that are easy to cut to final size (or are automatically cut with the right printer).

Rolls are really a necessity with panoramic image printing. "Pans," as people often call them, can vary considerably in their depth (top-to-bottom) compared to their width. Epson Stylus Photo printers can continuously print an image as deep as the printer's paper path is wide and 44 inches long.

You can also buy sheets of paper in big sizes for the larger ink jet printers, as well as for panoramics. These sheets are specific lengths cut to fit the width of the printer, for people not using roll holders. In addition, you can find sheets with unique tone and texture.

▲ **Some printers accept roll paper, which can be used for continuous printing of everything from 4 x 6 inch prints to panoramics.**

One-Manufacturer Convenience

Epson makes a diverse line of papers. This makes it very convenient and consistent for you because the printer driver (the software that controls the printer) includes settings directly linked to specific Epson papers.

There are some fine papers being made by a variety of sources, including some paper types that you can't get from Epson. Still, as much as possible, you will find it helpful to use Epson printing papers. Epson printers and their drivers are definitely optimized for these papers, which should come as no

surprise since the company has a lot invested in printer quality and wants buyers to get the best from the combination of printer, ink, and paper. You will also find that some independent papers that supposedly work well with all printers do not. This may result in weird effects as the ink pools in dark areas, for example.

In addition, Epson has created paper profiles for its paper products. We'll get into the technology of color management later for those readers interested in it. Briefly, you can set up color profiles for scanners, monitors, printers and paper so that your prints will look more like you expect. Epson even gives you profiles for its paper that can be "plugged in" to a color management workflow.

© Bob Krist

© Bob Krist

Photographer

Bob Krist

Travel Photography

One of the world's best-known travel photographers, **Bob Krist** shoots for a variety of travel magazines, such as *National Geographic Traveler, Smithsonian,* and *Islands*. He is also a contributing editor at both *National Geographic Traveler* and *Popular Photography* magazines.

He's been working with Epson printers since the late 1990s, and continues to use them for portfolio work, magazine submissions, gallery exhibits, and print sales. Krist uses a variety of papers, but tends to favor the matte finishes such as Epson's Enhanced Matte and a variety of fine art papers. For standard portfolio-type prints, he uses Epson's Premium Semi-Gloss paper. Overall, he's excited about the level of control the Epson products have given him.

For Krist, Epson ink jet printers have also opened up whole new areas for his business. For example, now he can sell his own art prints, which has given him a new income stream beyond being strictly an editorial photographer. In his mind, the quality/expense ratio is very, very good, since the Epson prints look as good as transparencies, and offer the chance to give a better presentation of his work.

When he's using the printers for proofing, Krist trusts the Epson printer to do its job well with just a little tweaking. Once he gets the prints to look like a transparency, he's happy—and proud. As he says, "If I want a picture up on my wall, 'bam'—there it goes. I don't have to sit in the dark and breathe bad fumes."

Web site: www.bobkrist.com

© Bob Krist

Technical Interlude

Can you skip the technical stuff and still get great prints? Actually, you can. However, photography has always been a mixture of technology and art. Getting the most from your printer does require you to understand some key technical details. This will not be an engineering discussion, though. I will try to bring the technical information back to relate to your primary purpose—making a print that truly satisfies you.

Mac vs. Windows

Okay, let's get this out of the way. Printers basically don't care where the data comes from. Photographic prints from an Epson printer look the same whether they start inside a Mac or Windows machine. In spite of the passionate arguments on both sides, for our purposes, there is no arbitrary better or worse to these excellent platforms. Both crash at times (although the most recent versions of operating systems in both do control this better), both can be either wonderful or a pain to deal with, and this can change in a matter of minutes.

The best computer platform for your printer really comes down to several things:

1 What platform do you use now and are you satisfied with it? If you are, there is no reason to change.

2 What do you use at work? You can either choose to continue to use something you are in constant contact with, or you can decide you might want something different, because it will be a break from work. It is not very hard to go back and forth between platforms after a short time of experience with either.

3 What do your friends use? It is best to use a computer platform of the same type as your immediate circle of friends and family. This way, you are more likely to get help and support when things don't work as they should (and sooner or later, this happens with any computer).

4 What are your software needs? If you have specific software needs that are only satisfied by one platform, then your choice is limited.

5 What style is aesthetically pleasing to you? There is a big range of computer designs in monitor and "box" (the CPU and computer guts).

◀ **Whether Mac or Windows platforms are used will not affect the appearance of the print, however, the printer interface is different for each.**

In this book, we don't specifically deal with either platform because it isn't necessary. There is nothing about ink jet printing that is unique to either Windows or Mac. Now, if you were a graphic designer, you might find some advantages to the Mac. Almost all commercial printing companies are set up to use the Mac; much fewer have any kind of Windows system. In many business settings, the Windows system has advantages because it has more software options.

The Printer Driver or Software

This unassuming part of printing, a partly automatic bit of software, is often taken for granted. Yet, it is a key part of the printing process. The wrong driver settings can totally change the look of your print. It can look like you spent some time readjusting it in your image-processing software, even though you never did.

The printer driver is the printing control part of your printer's software. Other elements of that software include such things as a utility to check ink levels, print head cleaning, alignment, and so forth. The printer driver comes up as soon as you tell the computer to print whatever is on your screen.

Once the printer driver comes up, you will find you need to make some simple, but extremely important, choices as to settings. The printer will automatically give you the right settings for a given paper, but you have to tell it what kind of paper you are printing on. Epson has worked very hard to develop complex algorithms (or computing instructions) to optimize your image when printed. These do their work quite well, but do require some simple choices in the printer driver.

Let's go through the key parts of the driver, as you would set it for printing. First, we'll do Windows then Mac, as they have different looking dialogue boxes, though the final choices are the same:

For Windows Users

1 Open the driver by going to the print part of your program's menu, to a printer icon, or if you use the keys, by using Ctrl P.

2 Be sure the correct printer is selected if you have more than one attached.

3 Click on Properties (**A**). In some software, there may be an additional window or dialogue box that comes up with a button that says Setup, Printer, or Options. You may need to click on those to tell the software how to deal with the photo it sends to the printer. The look of the driver interfaces can change, but their functionality remains essentially the same.

4 You should see the Properties dialogue box, labeled as such at the top.

▲ **A. Click on Properties in this Windows print dialogue box to get to the Epson printer driver.**

▲ **B. Choose the paper type to match the paper in the printer.**

▲ **C. PhotoEnhance settings are worth trying with digital camera files.**

▲ **D. TThe Paper Options tells the printer how to deal with the paper in use.**

▲ **E. The Layout section accesses special features.**

5 The Main section (**B**) asks you to choose the paper (Media Type), ink color, mode, and print preview. Choose a paper type that matches the paper in your printer. For all photographic printing, you will choose "color" for the ink color (even for black-and-white prints). For much of your printing, you will find that Epson has done such a good job optimizing its software that leaving the mode on automatic works great.

6 PhotoEnhance: You can also choose Photo-Enhance (**C**). This is a good setting to try with digital camera files that have had minimal modification because this setting will make some adjustments to the file to brighten and intensify the image. You can certainly try it on any photo, though. You will have some choices in this setting based on the type of photo and a couple of special effects. Again, Epson has done a lot of work to make this PhotoEnhance setting give you better prints. You probably won't use this mode if you are doing any significant corrections to the photo, but it only costs a sheet of paper to try if you aren't sure. This setting doesn't change the image file in the computer. Custom is an advanced setting that we will cover later.

7 For highest print quality, High Speed in the advanced section should not be checked. It is automatically set on Speed for plain paper, and for quick and easy photo printing, you might not notice much difference. If you see banding in

the print at all, this may be due to High Speed being checked.

8 Use the Print Preview by checking the box if you want to see the placement of the photo as it will appear on the page.

9 The Paper Options (**D**) gives some additional information to the printer. Here you let it know where the paper comes from (e.g., the standard sheet feeder or a roll feeder), the size of the paper (which is very important when you use anything other than the standard 8 ½ x 11), the image orientation (the printer needs to know if it is Portrait or Landscape) and how to use the area of the paper, Printable Area.

10 The Layout section (**E**) is a special area that accesses features for advanced users. It will let you adjust a photo to better use the page. If you have a file capable of printing larger than the paper, you can tell it to "Fit to Page" and the printer software will accommodate you.

You can also do some special printing, such as putting several pages on one (N-up)or making a poster bigger than the printer's size by using multiple pages. You can even add a special "Watermark" to clearly identify the photo as yours.

11 Click "Ok" to accept the settings, then click "Ok" on the first Print dialogue box.

For a Mac, the process is similar so read through the Windows section for some notes about settings that do apply to both platforms.

For Macintosh Users

1 Open the Page Setup option on the menu (**A**).

2 Be sure the correct printer is selected if you have more than one in use.

3 The Page Setup box is like the Paper section of the Windows driver. Here you tell the printer the size of the paper (which is very important when you use anything other than the standard 8 ½ x 11), where the paper comes from (e.g., the standard sheet feeder or a roll feeder), the image orientation (the printer needs to know if it is Portrait or Landscape) and how to use the area of the paper (Reduce/Enlarge and Printable Area).

4 Open the main printer driver (**B**) (you can just go to Print in the File menu). Now you need to choose the paper (Media Type), ink color, and mode. Choose a paper type that matches the paper in your printer (**C**). For all photographic printing, you will choose "color" for the ink color (even for black-and-white prints). For much of your printing, you may find that leaving the mode on automatic works great. You can also choose PhotoEnhance. See the section in Windows for more on this. Custom is an advanced setting that we will cover shortly.

5 The Speed/Quality slider in the mode area should be on Quality for photos. It is automatically on Speed for plain paper and can be set to speed if you want a quick print to check placement of a photo on a page, for example. It will print faster, but not at top quality, so should not be used to judge what a print would look like when it is printed at top quality.

6 Click "Print" to accept the settings and start printing.

EPSON

Letter
Normal
Color Controls

Copies: 1

Pages: ● All
○ Range [ ] ~ [ ]

Media Type: Photo Paper ▼

Ink
● Color
○ Black

Mode
● Automatic
○ PhotoEnhance
○ Custom

Quality ——⬤—— Speed
☐ EPSON Natural Color

? ▦ ▥ ▣ ▥ ▣   Print   Cancel

▲ **B.** Be sure the paper, ink color, and mode are chosen appropriately.

Plain Paper
360 dpi Ink Jet Paper
Photo Quality Ink Jet Paper
Matte Paper – Heavyweight
✓ **Photo Paper**
Premium Glossy Photo Paper
Photo Quality Glossy Film
Ink Jet Transparencies
Ink Jet Back Light Film

▲ **C.** Paper choices are critical to ensure the printer lays down ink properly.

Stylus Photo   (USB Port 1)

⏸ ▶ 🗑   Stop Print Queue   2 items   🗑

Photoshop 5.0 to 5.0.2 Log   User : EPSON
Copies : 1 / 1   Status : Processing job.
Pages : 1 / 2

Document Name	Priority	Paper Size	Media Type	Copies
mpagesetup	Hold	Letter	Plain Pa...	1

▽ Hide details

Document Name : mpagesetup
Priority : Hold ▼

Paper Size : Letter
Media Type : Plain Paper
Copies : 1
Pages : 1
User : EPSON
Orientation : Portrait
Watermark : None
Multi-Page : None

!

Working with your Epson printer driver is easy!

▲ The printer dialog box keeps you informed on the status of printing by displaying a list of documents being sent, or waiting to be sent, to the printer.

◀ **You adjust the color rendition tone options by choosing from Vivid, Photorealistic, or Automatic.**

◀ **Custom mode includes several options for color management.**

◀ **Advanced settings allow you to choose many of the printing settings that the Epson driver would otherwise set automatically.**

Custom or Advanced Settings

Epson has added a Custom settings button to its printer drivers in order to let you make more adjustments so your prints come out the way you want them. You'll find the start of this process in the Mode section of your printer driver. Select Custom and you'll see new choices. However, you may never need to access this part of the driver if you are getting what you want from your photos with the standard settings.

First, note one part of custom settings includes choices for ICM (Image Color Matching for Windows), RGB (standard Red Green Blue—Windows only) and ColorSync (Macintosh control). These are color management profiles that tie your printer closer to particular applications in the computer. At this point, you can try them and see if they help, but we'll get more into color management later.

The Advanced Settings choice can be very useful. It opens up a whole new set of possibilities for your printer. You can customize your settings such as Print Quality, Saturation, Color Balance, and Gamma and even save these settings. For most printing you can let the driver software choose this for you based on the paper type.

However, the Advanced Settings do let you control color in several ways. You can adjust the color saturation with the Mode choice (Automatic, Photorealistic, Vivid).The only way to see what they can do for you is to try them. Color adjustment can be very helpful in tweaking a print to make it look more like what you see on the monitor. We will cover this more in detail later in the book.

Gamma basically refers to the contrast of your printed image (not the image as displayed on the screen). Most of the time, you'll find the default setting, 1.8, works fine. You can try 1.5 to reduce the contrast of your print or 2.2 to increase it.

If you find that certain choices in Advanced Settings help with specific projects, like printing a brochure with multiple photos on a special paper, you can save these settings as a group. This allows you to go immediately to the same settings the next time you do the same type of printing.

Resolution

One issue that consistently comes to the attention of the editors of PCPhoto magazine is resolution. It is one of those subjects that causes headaches in the digital darkroom. Since something related to resolution affects every step from image capture (scanned or digital camera) through work in the computer to the actual print, we have to understand it to get the most from our prints.

In traditional photography, resolution is consistent. A lens, for example, could have its resolution checked and that resolution would not change. It would be nice if resolution worked the same through the whole digital process but unfortunately, it doesn't and this is where the confusion starts.

If you remember nothing else about resolution, always remember this: Image resolution and printer resolution are not the same. Photographers get into all sorts of trouble when they forget this. One of the most common printing problems is printing at the wrong image resolution. This shows up on the print as less sharpness, poor gradations of tone and color, less contrast, and weaker color.

▲ **The images above demonstrate the visual differences dependent upon the resolution. The large image (top left) is at 300dpi. The cropped image at top is printed at 150dpi, while the image just above is printed at 72dpi.**

The resolution of your image has a direct effect on the sharpness and quality of the print. Always remember that image resolution and printer resolution are not the same.

◀ **For the best print quality, set the resolution of your image to 200–300 dpi.**

Image Resolution

In order to get the best prints possible from your ink jet printer, you must start with the appropriate image resolution. Sure, the type of scanner or the brand of digital camera you use will have an affect on the resolution of the image file, but this is a secondary part of the equation and mainly affects how big you can make a print from a given file.

I'm going to give you a range to remember: 200–300. This refers to the image resolution needed for high-quality photo printing from your Epson printer, regardless of the printer resolution. Purists prefer to use the more accurate ppi (pixels per inch) for image resolution, but most people interchange it with dpi. While the two terms are slightly different, they essentially refer to the same thing.

I used to only recommend 300 ppi as the image resolution for printing, but this is a conservative number, especially with digital camera files. A 300 ppi file will print just fine, but using a lower number allows you to make a larger print from the same image file without interpolation. You may see references to 360 ppi, but this is an extremely conservative number. It works, but for all common photo printing situations, it offers no quality increase yet will dramatically increase the file size.

Image resolution always has two components: ppi and size. It is meaningless to know the number of pixels per inch without also knowing the image dimensions. This would be like saying someone went on a trip at 70 mph. Without knowing the travel time or distance, the 70mph has no point of reference. Check the image resolution and dimensions using the Image Size option of your software. Image browsers usually provide this information as well.

Digital cameras use pixel width and height to refer to image resolution (though technically, this was not how resolution was originally defined). For example, a six-megapixel camera has a maximum image size of 3072 x 2048 pixels, which gives a total area of just over 6,000,000 pixels.

It is important to remember that none of this relates to printer resolution. Image resolution is about the number of pixels in the digital file. The printer resolution is about putting dots of ink down on paper. Print quality may even decline if image resolutions higher than 400 ppi are used. Ink jet printers are not designed to print high resolution images, so more is not better once you've gone beyond the printer's optimum resolution.

Change resolution first with Resampling *not* checked.

Change picture size by keeping the resolution constant and checking Resample.

Adjusting Image Resolution

To adjust the image size and/or resolution, you'll need to open the Image Size dialogue box in your image-processing program and uncheck the Resample box. (Resampling changes the resolution by adding or deleting pixels to increase or decrease the size of a photo. Avoid resampling if possible.) This should link the image height, width, and resolution. Enter 200 ppi as the resolution to check the maximum print size you can make and 300 ppi to check the minimum size. If your desired print size falls in this range, just plug that size in and let the computer set the resolution. At this point, you are not adding or deleting pixels, which can affect image quality. However, you will need to resample the image if your photo is too big at 300 ppi or too small at 200 ppi. Check the Resample box and plug in new dimensions without changing the resolution.

What if you are looking at digital camera specifications that list the pixel height and width of a digital image file? You want to know what print size that digital camera is capable of. You can refer back to the 200–300 ppi recommendation to determine possible print sizes. For example, a 3072 x 2048 pixel image created by a six-megapixel camera would give a 10 x 15-inch print at 200 ppi and an

approximately 7 x 10-inch print at 300 ppi. You can quickly see why it is possible to make larger prints if you lower the image resolution. I'll explain how to do this in more detail in the next section.

Digital camera files enlarge quite well when you can't reach a desired print size with the native pixels. Photoshop CS and Photoshop Elements 3.0 offer newly enhanced enlargement algorithms to make this work even better. In addition, if you need to do a lot of image enlargement from the original file size, it helps to shoot RAW format files. RAW data enlarges slightly better than JPEG or TIFF files.

Image Guidelines

Print size	Minimum area resolution	
	(at 200 dpi)	(at 300 dpi)
4 x 6 in	800 x 1200	1200 x 1800
5 x 7 in	1000 x 1400	1500 x 2100
8 x 10 in	1600 x 2000	2400 x 3000

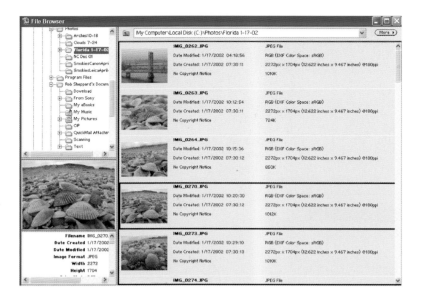

▲ File browsers provide a lot of information about image files, including the image resolution, area resolution, and file size of a photo. This file browser is part of Adobe Photoshop Elements.

Resolution and Print Sizes

Once you start understanding resolution, you'll be able to see how much resolution you will need in a scanned photo in order to make a certain size print, or how many megapixels you'll need from a digital camera. You'll also be able to look at a photo's area resolution to tell how big a print can be made. Multiply the dimensions of a print in inches (such as 8 x 10) times 300 (an easy number to use for dpi) and you will get the area resolution needed. For the 8 x 10, this would be 2400 x 3000 total pixels, 2400 on the eight inch side, 3000 on the ten inch side.

So you need an area resolution of 2400 x 3000. If your image has significantly less than this, it will not make a great straight print to 8 x 10. It will need to be magnified through pixel interpolation where the pixels are spread out, and then the gaps between them are filled by the computer's intelligent guesses as to what belongs in between.

You can get there in several ways. You could use a digital camera with a high enough resolution. Technically, this would be about a 7-megapixel camera, but actually smaller digital camera files will print well to this size. Still, they must be enlarged and sharpened in an image-processing program for best results. You'll see this in the resize and resample commands of many programs.

With a film scanner, this means you'd need a minimum of 2400 dpi for a 35mm scan. The narrow side is one inch, so all of the pixels needed for the full eight inches of the 8 x 10 (2400) have to fit into this one inch. With a flatbed, you'd need 600 dpi for a 4 x 6 (you need to get all 2400 pixels on the short side out of four inches or 4 x 600) or 300 dpi for an 8 x 10. In this case, the printing size is the same as the scanned size, so a print at 300 dpi requires 300 dpi for the scan.

You should note that the smaller the original image compared to the printing size, the higher the resolution needed for scanning. The only way to make an image bigger in the computer is to increase pixels, by scanning at a higher resolution, using a higher megapixel camera or having the computer interpolate pixels. The first two are always preferable to the third, because with them the pixels correspond to real things (whether elements of film or a print for a scan or parts of a scene with a digital camera) rather than being made up by the computer (interpolation).

Printer Resolution

Epson printers come with several resolutions: 360, 720, 1440, 2880, and 5760 dpi. Let me repeat this very important concept: printer resolution and image resolution are two different things. If you were to try to make an 8 x 10 print, for example, with an image resolution of 1440 dpi, you'd see a reduction in print quality and a terrible slowdown of your computer at the minimum, and in the worst case, a complete crash of the system. Also remember: printer resolution is not enough to define the highest quality in a print.

You will actually see printer resolution listed as two numbers, such as 1440 x 720 or 2880 x 1440. The first number is very important in looking at resolution, but the second number is critical for highest quality, as it refers to how the ink jet head actually puts these ink droplets down in the second dimension of printing. Since printing makes a two-dimensional print, the second number actually fills in the ink in the second direction.

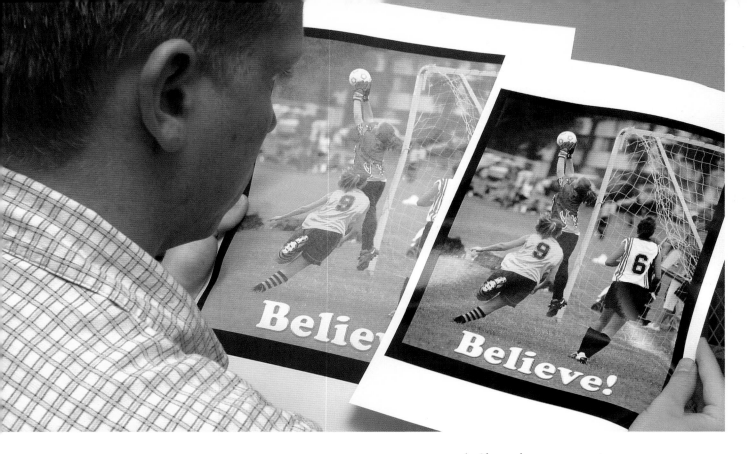

▲ Always be sure you set your printer driver and resolution settings correctly. The difference between using a right or wrong setting can be quite dramatic.

Your Epson printer will automatically set the correct dpi for the paper used as long as you set your printer driver correctly by choosing the appropriate paper setting. If you go to the custom/advanced settings, you'll be able to choose the exact printer dpi you want for a specific purpose. The higher the dpi, the better small details are rendered and tonal changes (the gradations between colors) are improved. For most photo printing, you may find that 1440 gives you results hard to distinguish from higher resolutions. In addition, higher dpi also means slower printing and more ink is used.

360 is fast, but not a photo-quality setting. 720 and up are photo-quality choices. For many purposes, you may find that 720 dpi is a good compromise between quality and speed, especially on matte papers. Try it and see what you like. 1440 gives the very high photographic quality that Epson printers are known for. 2880 and 5760 are slightly better, but the difference may be hard to see on many photos. Where this may show up is in subtle highlights and shadow detail on glossy paper. However, the time required to print at the higher dpi's goes up dramatically and may not be worth the effort on most photos.

Crashes

I mentioned that trying to print at very high image resolutions can cause crashes. This is because the large image files stress the computer's resources. It is almost as if the computer has trouble figuring out where to put all that data: in RAM in a temp file, or on the hard drive? So rather than dealing with that, because a computer is too smart to be bothered with such mundane tasks, it just says forget it and crashes.

Of course, the technical reasons behind this are far more complex. But the point is that big photo files are most likely to cause crashes. This is not un-common when printing, because the computer needs processing power, (RAM and hard drive space) to be able to process a file for printing. If you seem to have consistent crashes when working with photos, try adding more RAM to your system, (moving it up to 256 MB or more). This frequently solves the problem.

© George Lepp

George Lepp

Nature Photographer and Master Teacher

As the Field Editor for *Outdoor Photographer* and *PC Photo* magazines, **George Lepp** is one of the most widely respected nature photography experts in the business. He also directs the Lepp Institute of Digital Imaging, and conducts seminars across the country on outdoor photography and the digital darkroom. His extensive experience in location photography gives Lepp a teaching perspective that few other photographers can match.

He's used Epson products since the introduction of Epson's first photo printer. Today he uses them both for his own high-quality prints and as teaching aids for his students, so they can learn to master the digital darkroom.

Lepp relies on several models of Epson printers, from the smaller desktop units to the wide-format printers. He enjoys experimenting with a range of different papers, but prefers Epson's Luster paper for general printing, and watercolor papers for most of his display prints.

© George Lepp

Epson printers and the computer have given what Lepp calls the "second half of photography" back to photographers. "Before, once the photograph was taken, working on a color image was difficult for the average photographer. Now there's complete control from start to finish." For example, he can now optimize different aspects of his image in the computer—and in the print. "Using the image I captured as a starting point, I can now make it closer to what I saw in the subject, or I can change things around and experiment," Lepp says. "And I can print them immediately to see how they turn out, which is better than sending out a transparency for printing. Prints seldom match the transparency anyway."

For Lepp, new printing technology has become a wonderful tool to ignite a joy and passion for photography in ways never before possible. He embraces the technology as it evolves, and encourages his students to do so as well. For example, he is a fan of Epson's new UltraChrome ink set, since it gives him an incredible color gamut combined with long-lasting print life—opening new possibilities for creative expression.

More on Lepp and his classes and workshops can be found at www.leppphoto.com.

Refining the Image for Printing— Image-Processing Programs

What do you expect from your photographs? A nice likeness? A photo that looks real? A print that you can be proud of? An image that says something special about your subject?

All of these are reasons that we take photos and make prints. And to really get the most out of these images, we now have some wonderful things we can do in the digital darkroom, the computer. You will find that some photos require a lot of work to look their best, yet others may require little or nothing. I don't spend a lot of time on every photo that I print, and I wouldn't expect you to do that either.

Sometimes you just need a quick and easy print for reference or to give a friend or relative. When the original was shot on a digital camera you can simply use an Epson direct printer. Then again, you'll often find that a print can be made much more satisfying with a quick tweak of brightness or color.

I want to give you some ideas on how to work with an image-processing program to create an image that will give you a print that will satisfy you. Now I do recognize that having lots of controls in an image-processing program can make folks want to try everything and not necessarily be happy with any of it. Hopefully, these next few chapters will offer you a little different look at how you might control an image so that you will be able to make the prints you want.

There are many good programs on the market today for adjusting photos. Adobe Photoshop is probably the best known and does offer some superb features. However, it is expensive and has a steep learning curve. Photoshop Elements can do nearly as much for the average photographer, but for less money and time investment. Photoshop is very powerful and worth the investment for those photographers who need it. However, this is not an issue of quality—both are high-quality programs. Photoshop simply offers some specialized tools that are worthless to someone who does not need them, and absolutely essential to those who do.

There are other excellent programs on the market, from Jasc Paint Shop Pro to Ulead PhotoImpact. Nothing in the next two chapters is specific to any one program.

Once you discover the possibilities of what you can do in the digital darkroom, your print options increase, along with the possibility of making really stunning prints that satisfy your deepest creative urges.

Jasc Paint Shop Pro is a low-priced, menu-based program with a great deal of power.

Photoshop Elements 3 (below) is a good basic image-processing program designed to make adjustments easy for photographers.

Some programs are designed to change images into new creative forms. Corel IX is a very adaptable program for creating painting-like images from photos or from scratch.

Adobe Photoshop (below) is a very powerful menu-based program with a steeper learning curve.

But the Software is Overwhelming!

I'm going to let you in on a secret that I share in my workshops and magazine articles. You don't have to know everything about how a program works in order to use it to make beautiful prints. Unfortunately, a lot of books try to cover it all so that every last detail of a program is unearthed.

No matter what program you use, you are the photographer and your photo is the important thing, not the program. It doesn't matter how many filters a program offers, for example, if you only use two. If your photo looks great after simply adjusting the brightness and contrast, you've done just the right thing!

You're the photographer; you're the one making the prints. Learn, experiment, and work to make your images better, but trust in your judgment. You're the only one who can ultimately decide if a print should be lighter or darker, not other photographers, not computer software engineers, not Photoshop gurus with a need for control.

Learn the software in bits. Master each part as you go. But never worry if you don't know it all. Few do.

Image-Processing Software

So what is the best image-processing program? Every year we try to address this in *PCPhoto* magazine's annual buyer's guide. I honestly don't believe there is one best program, appropriate for everyone. A better question might be: "Which is the best program for what I want to do?"

First, never simply pick a program based on how many features it has. If you don't need certain features, ignore them. Look at a program's features in terms of what might be useful to you. This may be hard if you're a beginner. In that case, start simply with an easy-to-use program even if it doesn't have everything possible.

Second, every program has a certain "personality" that comes across in its interface and how it works. You can get an idea of personality based on how the program is promoted on the software box, by checking the manufacturer's Web site and by seeing whether the program is button/icon- or menu-based.

Any program is going to work its best with someone who spends the time to master it and the craft of the digital darkroom. I guarantee that my 14-year-old daughter will do better with Microsoft Picture It!, which she knows well, than a neophyte on Photoshop.

One way of categorizing programs is to look at how most actions are initiated. Are they icon or button-based with lots of step-by-step elements, or they are menu-based programs? The button-based, step-by-step programs are generally very accessible and usable right away. They usually are very strong on easy-to-use basic controls, special effects, and printing capabilities. Even sophisticated power users will use these programs for quick and easy printing jobs or for printing special projects.

Menu-based programs offer more power with greater choices. Power and choices are a double-edged sword. While they allow you to do some very advanced image editing, they also require more time dealing with a sometimes-steep learning curve. Photoshop Elements offers a nice compromise with its Hints palette and intuitive groupings of controls.

Lets look at some of the key photographic features that definitely can affect your printing, features that photographers consistently use with photos on their computers. I'll give you a quick list, and then we'll look more in depth at two very important groups of features and how they can help you make better prints.

15 key features to look for in an image-processing program:

1
Brightness/Contrast
Most programs offer a simple set of sliders to adjust how dark or light an image is, as well as its contrast. While very intuitive, these adjustments are heavy-handed and have less flexibility than other controls.

2
Levels
This is a brightness/contrast or "exposure" tool that offers excellent control over adjustments. You can affect the dark, light, and middle tones separately.

3
Curves
An advanced brightness/contrast or "exposure" tool that allows great flexibility because you can make small adjustments to the image's many tones.

4
Hue/Saturation
A tool to adjust the color balance (hue) and color richness or intensity (saturation) of an image.

5
Color Balance control
An intuitive color adjustment that subtly changes the color balance of an image along three scales: cyan to red, green to magenta and yellow to blue.

6
Layers
A key tool for separating adjustments and alterations to an image by isolating them into layers stacked one on top of another. It is well worth the extra work needed to understand and use layers.

7
Adjustment layers
Layers of instructions that tell the program how to adjust underlying (and unchanged) layers.

8
Layer masks
A control that allows you to turn parts of a layer on or off as needed; always used with adjustment layers; can be added to layers in other programs.

9
Layer modes
Unique ways that layers communicate with each other to build new effects.

10
Multiple selection tools
Tools of varying shapes and methods available for selecting all or part of an image.

11
Clone tool
A specialized select-and-copy tool that duplicates or moves a section of the image from one spot to another; for retouching or to cover flaws.

12
Dodge/Burn tools
Special brushes that lighten (dodge) and darken (burn) areas of the image.

13
Unsharp Mask
A highly controllable form of sharpening that includes amount, radius, and threshold.

14
Gaussian Blur
A very manageable, specific type of blur.

15
Multiple picture printing
Printing options that allow you to put more than one picture on a page.

Refining the Image for Printing– Tonal Adjustments

Most people know of Ansel Adams and his wonderful black-and-white landscape photos. He used to spend days in the darkroom making those images just right. Though Adams essentially only had two controls, he could change the photo's brightness and its contrast. He would "apply" those controls to effect the tonal range of the entire image, or selectively adjust small parts of the photo isolated from the rest.

With just those two controls, he created prints that made him famous. Getting a good print is a craft, whether you do it in the darkroom or with your Epson printer. As you try different adjustments, you'll discover many exciting possibilities with your prints. This is why I really believe that the so-called experts who want to make the process an engineering exercise in computer technology are misguided. Adams always looked at a finished print and studied it to see if it was what he wanted. If it wasn't quite right, he made some new adjustments and made a new print. He often took days doing that. We have the huge advantage of doing this in minutes.

There are three brightness/contrast or "exposure" controls: Brightness/Contrast, Levels, and Curves. You may use all of them over time, although with practice, you will find each control has its benefits for making adjustments to images.

The Simple Brightness/ Contrast Control

Every image-processing program that I know of has this control. They are grouped together since it is rare to adjust one and not the other. The controls, usually simple sliders, make separate adjustments for Brightness and Contrast.

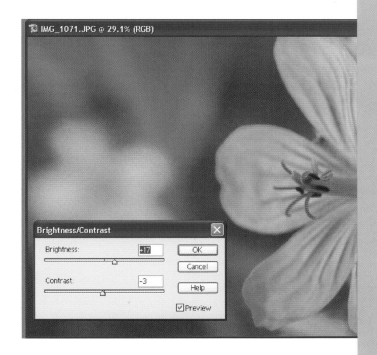

▲ **Brightness/Contrast is a simple, intuitive control that can be used for basic adjustments.**

Brightness/Contrast is one of those controls that Photoshop snobs will tell you should never be used. While it's true that this is a "blunt instrument" sort of control, as a basic and intuitive adjustment it works well for the photographer new to image processing. It is certainly the quickest and easiest way of altering image brightness and contrast. You simply make an image brighter or darker, more or less contrasty, by adjusting the sliders accordingly. It's an easy change that makes the photo look the way it should or the way you think it looks best.

This control is one that most photographers outgrow because of its limitations. It makes the entire image brighter or darker, less or more contrasty, without any finesse or fine tuning. Levels and Curves both offer much more flexibility and control over image adjustments and allow you to more carefully control the black and white points in a photo. (This can be critical to making a good print, as explained in the next section.) Still, Brightness/Contrast is a useful tool when you need to make a quick and easy change to an image.

▲ **Push your controls beyond the normal adjustment ranges so you can get a better idea of what they can do. Crank them to the extreme—you can always "Undo" everything. You can't hurt the image.**

The Extreme Thing

I've found in classes and workshops that many photographers have an overwhelming tendency to make only subtle adjustments to a photo. They ease on through the tweaking process, almost afraid to do too much.

You can't go too far as long as you don't tell the computer to print or save! Take that control and really crank it. See what it will do. Push it to the extreme so you can see what the adjustment really does to a photo. Then back it off to where it looks good.

Form a habit of doing this. Making adjustments that go beyond what you need, then pulling the adjustment back to where it looks good is, I believe, the best way to make first adjustments to a photo. If you tweak a little, then a little more, then a bit more, and so on, each adjustment is so small that you never really see the difference. So you have a tendency to over adjust. Or if you quit too soon, under adjust. Of course you can refine your adjustments to get the best print, but if you haven't taken the "Extreme Thing" approach to start, you'll find those refinements harder to do. Whenever you get stuck and are not sure what needs to be done to a photo, try this "Extreme Thing" technique. It will often be just the thing to get you going.

Levels and Why Black and White Are So Important

A key adjustment tool for photographers is Levels. This may seem a little intimidating at first. After all, it does seem to be more about graphs than photography. Yet, this tool can be the most important Brightness/ Contrast control you have for making better prints.

To understand why Levels can be so helpful, you need to understand the importance of solid black and solid white in a print. All good darkroom printers usually strive to have something pure black and something pure white in their print (the exceptions are gray conditions like fog). These create reference points for the eye. We subconsciously note the pure black and pure white parts of an image to tell us what the tones (the steps of brightness between black and white) of an image are.

A print without both will look dull and gray, without the crispness and brilliance modern cameras are capable of capturing. Epson printers, with their use of a photo-optimized black in the ink set, give an extremely dense black that makes the photos look crisp and rich. However, if your image does not

have a pure black, the printer can't print this wonderful tone.

The Levels control tells us immediately if we have this total range of tones from pure white to pure black. You don't have to be a math expert to figure this out. The graph that comes with Levels, called the histogram, shows the proportions of pixels, from black to white, left to right. The blacks are on the far left and there is a little black triangle below. The whites are on the far right and a little white triangle takes up residence underneath. The rest of the picture is graphed in between—all the midtones.

The histogram needs to start rising on the left and finish on the right. If it doesn't and there is a gap on the left and no part of the graph makes it to the edge, there are no solid blacks in the photo. If there is a gap on the right, so that it doesn't touch the far white side, then the highlights will gray. To adjust, you simply move the black slider on the left, until it is under the start of the histogram, and move the white slider on the right until it is under the end of the histogram.

▲ A good print requires a full tonal range from black to white. Levels helps you set that range. The graph here is called a histogram and can be used to set the black and white levels in a photo. (Compare photos at left and right).

This then can become an automatic way of checking to see if you will have good blacks in your print—always be sure there are blacks and whites in your image by checking levels. You don't have to stop here. You can continue to move the black and white sliders toward the center, either separately or together, to create contrast in your image. The neat thing about levels is that you can create this contrast by favoring the dark areas (left, black slider) or the light areas (right, white slider) in your adjustments.

As you make your changes to the image, the midtones, the bulk of the image, will also change. You can make them lighter or darker by moving the midtone, gray slider in the middle to the left or to the right. This is a very powerful way of dealing with an image. The midtones can now be brightened or darkened, as appropriate to your vision of the subject, without affecting the blacks or whites.

The result of all this individual adjusting is that you can control the shadow, middle-gray or highlight areas without changing the other areas as much. This is a tremendous tool for the creative photographer who really wants something special from his or her prints.

Photoshop and Photoshop Elements offer the Eyedropper tool for help in setting the black and white points, as well as a neutral tone. Although some workers find them helpful, I rarely use them. They seem rather arbitrary to my taste. I prefer to do my own setting of black and white.

To use levels, first set the black (left slider) and white (right slider) points by moving those sliders to the start of the graph. Then adjust the middle slider (gamma or mid-tones) to make the photo lighter or darker.

▲ The Levels histogram can be used to determine if exposure is adequate. A good exposure (whether from a digital camera or film that is scanned) makes your work easier and gives better images for printing. The photo above is underexposed and doesn't have the full range of tones or information found in the bottom image.

Curves

Curves is another graphic adjustment tool that can help you adjust the brightness and contrast of an image. Some Photoshop experts prefer to use Curves alone. I find that this is not useful to the average photographer. Setting a strong black and white, as described in the Levels section, is something photographers can relate to. While black and white points can be set with the eyedroppers that come with Curves, this can also alter the color balance of your photograph.

I open Levels first, set the black and white points in the image, and then check to see if a slight adjustment of the midtone Levels slider will give me the results I want. Very often, this provides acceptable overall exposure control for a print. But if you need to make more than a slight adjustment of that midtone slider, Curves will usually give better results. And in other situations, if adjustment of the midtone slider will not make your image look the way you want—then you really do need Curves.

I will still set the black and white points first with Levels because of the control I get and the ability to retain subtle and important color casts. Then I open Curves. The Curves dialogue box shows a graph with a diagonal line running from the lower left to upper right corner. Points on the line represent the tones in

the image from black (lower left) to white (upper right). You can click on any point on the line and drag the curve up to lighten the image or down to darken it. This creates very smooth tonal changes from the maximum (where you clicked and dragged) to minimum (where the line hits the corners).

I first concentrate on the midtones by clicking the line in the center and moving it up (to lighten) or down (to darken). If I need to lighten dark areas more, I would adjust a point to the left of the center. If I need to darken light areas more, I would click to the right. You can select multiple points on the line to adjust different tones separately. Sometimes it only takes a small movement of the line to make a significant change to your photo. Use the arrow keys to make small, precise movements.

Selections

By selecting a specific area of your photo and isolating your adjustment controls to that section, you can totally change whatever is inside the selected area without effecting adjacent pixels (even something right next to the selected area, but outside the selection). You can choose a discreet part of an image by outlining areas with a Selection tool. This can be a powerful control for making that masterful print that needs a little darkening or lightening in one area.

All of the Selection tools can be useful, from the shaped selection tools (rectangles and circles) to the freehand Lassos (which follow your cursor) to the very helpful automatic tools (the Magnetic Lasso and the Magic Wand, for example). With any of these, you move your cursor around the area to be selected and a selection line will appear (some people call this the marching ants). Making good selections can be tricky. This really is an eye-hand-coordination thing that takes some practice.

◀ **Curves is a special tool that allows you to adjust specific tones to fine-tune an image. It can isolate changes to light or dark areas of the image.**

▲ Selections can help you adjust specific areas of a photo. Here, the beetle was selected. The selection was feathered to blend it, and inverted so that everything except the beetle was selected. The outside was darkened to give visual emphasis to the beetle.

Selection tips

1 Enlarge your image, so that you can better see edges of your subject. You need to see in order to determine where your selection should go.

2 Don't worry if the initial selection isn't perfect. You can both add and subtract from the selection in order to refine it. Usually, you will hold down the shift key as you make selections to add to the area, and the alt or option key to subtract.

3 Use more than one Selection tool. Use whatever seems to work best for you, in whatever order you find helpful. Just remember to use the shift or alt/option keys to add or subtract.

4 Look for easy ways to select. If you can use an automatic tool (such as the Magic Wand on the sky), use it to select a background, then invert the selection to capture the desired area.

5 When you have made your selection, feather it. Feathering is a blending or smoothing of the selection edge. Selected edges are generally much sharper than those that would naturally occur in a photograph. Feathering takes that edge off. How much is totally dependent on the photo, so experiment. I find it easiest to control and experiment with feathering when I do it to a selection rather than adding it to the Selection tool.

Dodge and Burn

I mention the Dodge and Burn tools last in this chapter, not because they aren't useful, but because they should be used sparingly to make the final refinements to the brightness and contrast of an image. They were key in the traditional darkroom, but because we have so much control in the digital darkroom, our computer, it is often easier and more effective to darken and lighten parts of an image by using selections.

Dodge and Burn are "painting" tools, meaning that you use them as you would a brush. You must choose the right size brush and how strong you want the effect. Generally, you'll find a setting of 10-15% is plenty. You are better off applying dodging and burning in steps rather than trying to do it all at once. The latter tends to look splotchy and rather artificial. In addition, you can choose whether to favor shadows, midtones, or highlights.

You'll find dodging is great to brighten small areas, such as the whites of eyes or teeth (be careful you don't overdo it, though), highlights in a waterfall or hair, and so forth. Look at your image on the screen first, then your test prints later, to see if you can't make a print a little livelier by whitening some light areas. Use selections to control large areas, as both dodging and burning can look splotchy if done too hard over big areas.

Burn areas that need darkening. This can be very helpful to strengthen local contrast, such as a shadow on one side of your subject or the dark rocks of a waterfall. It can make a subject stand out against a background by either darkening the background around it or burning the subject's edge. Often you will find that, if you make a selection along the edge you need to darken, then use that selection to control your burning, you'll be better able to darken just what needs it. If you then invert the selection, you'll be able to dodge/lighten the other side of the edge as well.

▲ **Dodge tools let you lighten and burn tools let you darken small areas of an image. Here they were used to enhance the flow of the water.**

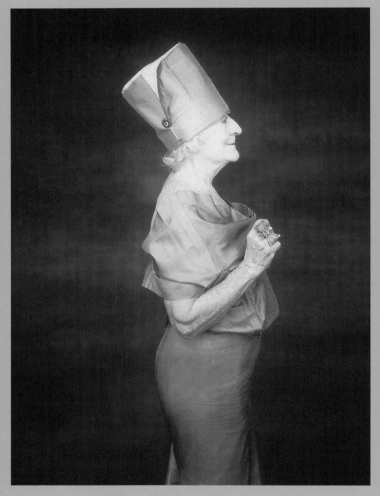

© Joyce Tenneson, from *Wise Women*

© Joyce Tenneson, from *Wise Women*

Photographer

Joyce Tenneson

© Lisa Devlin

Balancing Assignments and Personal Work

Joyce Tenneson is a highly acclaimed photographer known for her powerful portraits. She has been the recipient of many awards, including the International Center of Photography's Infinity Award. She has also been voted by *American Photo* readers as among the 10 most influential women photographers in the history of photography. And she has achieved commercial success, with cover photos for magazines such as *Time, Esquire,* and *Premiere.*

Tenneson has a unique style that requires an ability to capture subtle nuances and feels the Epson printers deliver. "I use Epson printers as tools to achieve my artistic vision. The prints that are produced can include nuances that differentiate a good photograph from a great photograph. In addition, having a quality printer in the studio gives me the freedom to try out different things, and get the best image I possibly can. I have infinitely more options now than I did before."

She began working with Epson printers over five years ago, and now relies heavily on them, using both desktop and wide-format models. Beyond their incredible image quality, they also provide the permanence she needs for her fine art photographs.

Tenneson also feels the Epson printers are versatile. When asked which type of work she uses ink jet prints for, she responds with enthusiasm, "Everything! I deliver aim prints to clients and produce prints for exhibition." Epson printers were also involved in the production of her most recent book, *Wise Women.*

Like all pros, she feels that the photo paper used in the printer makes a big difference in the prints, and her soft tonalities often lend themselves well to papers that are not glossy. She especially likes the Epson heavyweight matte papers.

There is no question that, for Tenneson, Epson ink jet printers have revolutionized her studio. She believes they have given her more control of the technical part of the process, freeing her up to concentrate on her creativity. As she puts it, "Ink jet printing will take over the photo industry."

Tenneson's work can be seen at:
www.joycetenneson.com.

Refining the Image for Printing– Color Adjustments

In the traditional darkroom, black-and-white was king. While you could adjust a color print, it was hard to do. It required the use of toxic chemicals, had to be done in total darkness, and would take a substantial amount of time. Getting a good color print was sometimes a challenge, even when you went to a lab. In addition, many people shot color slides (especially the pros), which could be printed as photographs, but not all labs did a good job with them.

So, many photographers got the idea that color could not be changed. You picked the film you liked and just went with it. Wow, has that idea become outdated. With the digital darkroom, we have wonderful control over color, and as we saw in the last chapter, it starts with Brightness/Contrast controls. You could never change a color print before as we can today with the controls available in Levels.

Color and the "Good" Print

What is good color in a print? Something that matches what's on the monitor? Not necessarily. Color that matches what's on a slide? That doesn't mean it's real. Color that looks real? Sometimes. How about color that is pure without being muddied by unwanted colorcasts?

I believe that good color in a print is color that satisfies you and your unique rendition of the subject. A scientist who needs precise matching of hues to the real-world subject will have very different needs than a wildly creative artist-type who pushes the limits of photography. Probably most of us fit somewhere in between.

Regardless of where you are on such a spectrum, you know better than anyone else what you like. Don't be intimidated by what some "expert" says about the way you are making prints if you like the results. Printmaking is a personal craft, always has been, and I believe, always should be. As you make more and more prints, some will be good, some bad, but you will learn and refine your work like any craftsperson. Books and classes can help you learn new tools, but ultimately, you know what you like and dislike. Have fun making prints and be proud of your photos as they come alive for you in a print.

Printing should be fun and playful. That's always been a part of creativity and certainly printmaking with an ink jet printer should be creative.

Here are some ideas you can use to evaluate the color of your image on screen and when it is printed.

1 **Remove annoying color casts**—Color casts can be beautiful, such as the golden tones at sunset, but they can also be a problem with photos, when the colors annoy you and distract from the subject. A picture can pick up such colors from the light (such as fluorescent), the scanning process, or even digital camera bias in certain lighting conditions. This cast is usually most noticeable in neutral colors such as gray and white.

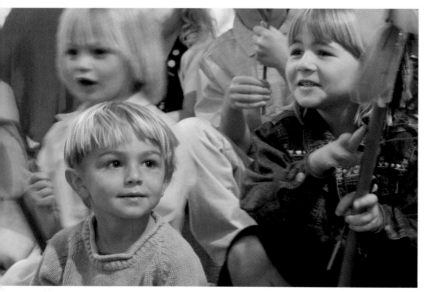

▲ Strong color casts can result from many lighting conditions. Color Variations or Color Balance controls can help you correct them.

▲ Often, key colors are the most important part of a print and need the most attention to getting them right.

2 **Evaluate key colors**—Often you will find that certain colors dramatically impact the print. Their effect on the photo is far greater than their relative portion of the image. Examples might be a particular blue sky, a patch of yellow flowers, the red in a soccer player's jersey and so forth. These are colors that are very important to the subject, to the composition, to the mood, or any other aspect of the photo. They are so important that, if this color were missing, the photo would not work. These key colors are well worth spending time adjusting.

3 **Watch out for contaminated colors**—Some colors are more susceptible to contamination than others. By contamination, I mean that the colors become less pure and pick up other hues that really don't belong. You can look for contamination in any color, but the following colors tend to exhibit this problem: yellow (yellow degrades quickly to green or red), blue sky (often picks up too much red), blue flowers (film is over-sensitive to ultraviolet light which tends to make blue flowers too red, or purple), pale colors (these are often influenced by other nearby colors), and dark green (this can pick up red which makes it dark and muddy).

4 **Consider the vividness or saturation of the colors**—Colors make us react in part because of their emotional quality. That often is the result of the saturation of colors, how vivid the color is. You can find colors that are too vivid (say a red wall behind a woman with strawberry blonde hair—the red wall will overpower the hair) or you can also find colors are too dull (for example, brightly colored flowers on a gray, cloudy day).

5 **Evaluate color rendition**—The difference between vivid and muted color prints is not just a matter of subject but more of personal style or taste. Some people consistently prefer more vividly colored prints, while others want something gentler. Neither is correct, but once you realize that you have such preferences, you can work to make your prints consistently express them.

6 **Compare color relationships within the image**—Colors rarely are seen on their own. Almost always, they interact with other colors around them. Consequently, they interact with each other in your photo. Look at them. Is a red overpowering gentler colors? Are grays too light and pulling color out of an isolated subject? Think about how the image would look if certain colors were made stronger, weaker, or different. One powerful change is to increase the color saturation of foreground colors, for example, and decrease the saturation in the background.

7 **Consider what looks real**—You've probably heard people say that a bizarre news event could never be made into a movie because no one would believe it. This actually happens in our photos, too. Your print may actually look just like the slide, and you may believe the slide is an accurate rendition of the world as you saw it. Still, a photo must "read" as real, meaning the viewer must believe it is real, if that is the result you want. You'll sometimes find that some colors just don't seem to have a real feel to them. Trust your intuition and adjust until you are satisfied.

8 **Consider color alternatives**—Sometimes it is fun to make photos with wild and exotic colors. Go for it! Have some fun with alternative colorings of your image. However, to be effective, you generally need to make strong changes in the colors. Subtle differences with alternative colors will look more like a mistake than a creative choice.

◀ **Colors don't always photograph or print true to the original. Hue/Saturation can help you adjust them.**

Hue/Saturation

Almost every image-processing program lets you affect hue (the actual spectral color) and saturation (intensity). Usually, there will be a slider control for hue, which allows you to change colors. You can get wild effects with this. You can also select a specific part of a photo, for example, a red flower, and adjust its hue, or even change the color altogether.

Saturation is a key color tool. This allows you to change the intensity of colors. You can adjust the whole photo to make colors more or less saturated. It is not unusual to find that you like a print to have a different saturation than what you like on the screen. That is the nature of prints. In addition, you will find that different papers give different color renditions, especially in the area of saturation, so this control is always helpful.

Over the years, photographers have been drawn to the brighter, more intense films, both slides and prints. Kodak even markets a film called Extra Color. Yet, digital cameras often produce files that print with less color intensity. Try bumping the saturation up 10-15% and see if that helps.

The Hue/Saturation adjustment window usually includes a "Lightness" setting as well, which should be used only for slight tweaking of colors due to changes in saturation.

In a number of programs, you can actually isolate the Hue/Saturation adjustments to a particular color. In Adobe Photoshop and Photoshop Elements, for example, you can click next to where it says Edit: Master and a drop down menu will appear with specific colors. If you then move the cursor onto the photo, it will turn into an Eyedropper. Click on the appropriate color in the photo and the adjustments will be specific to that color.

▲ You can control how a viewer looks at your print by adjusting color saturation in the Hue/Saturation dialogue box, even down to adjusting mainly a single color.

▲ Variations uses visual references to help you adjust color. Click on the photo you like among the color and exposure choices.

Color Balance and Variations

Frequently, a photo will be just a little off in color, sort of like a song that is sung slightly off key. It will never print satisfactorily. Color Balance controls and the Variations adjustments available in many programs can definitely come to the rescue.

Color Variations in versions 2 and 3 of Photoshop Elements is a very intuitive set of controls that uses three thumbnails to control the amount of red, green, and blue in a photo. You can set the adjustment window to favor shadows, midtones or highlights. The thumb-nails are set up to add or reduce the computer colors, red, green, and blue (RGB). You'll often find it works best with the intensity set low.

In Color Balance, sliders control the amount of red, green, and blue intensity in a photo. Again, you can set the adjustment window to favor shadows, mid-tones, or highlights. The sliders are set up with complementary colors—cyan to red, green to magenta, yellow to blue—or they are set up to add more or less of the computer colors, red, green, and blue (RGB).

Either way, just click on thumbnails or move sliders to make the colors look more like you expect them to look. There is no right or wrong to this. The key is to look at your image on the screen, then later as a print, and think about how it appears to you. I strongly recommend using the Extreme Thing technique, described in the previous chapter, to see what colors need most adjustment.

▲ Digital cameras often need a slight boost in color saturation. Try adding 10-15% to start.

▲ The colors of a photo can be rendered as neutral, warm, or cold in tone. For many images, the warm tones are most appealing.

Either color balance control is especially useful with photos shot in the shade or on cloudy days, when the light is mixed, or under fluorescent lights. Frequently, images shot in the shade or on a cloudy day lack warmth, although they may or not look overly blue. In this case, add yellow and red (or remove blue and cyan) until the image looks right to you. Skin tones, especially, start to glow nicely with added warmth.

When the light is mixed, such as in a photograph taken near a window, that also includes light from an incandescent lamp, colors can appear unreal in pictures taken with film or digital cameras. You may even find that part of the photo is too warm while another part is too blue. In this case, you need to make a selection of one area at a time, feather the selection (this smoothes the edge), then adjust the color balance of the selected area.

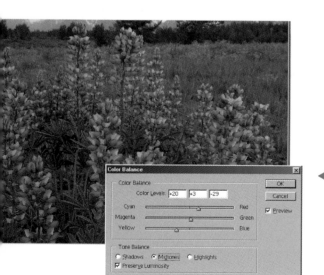

◀ Add the effect of using a warming filter by increasing the red and yellow in the photo through Color Balance.

Fluorescent lights have an incomplete spectrum of color, and tend to cause a greenish cast in pictures shot with film. With digital capture, fluorescents can either give sort of natural color (which may be okay or require only minor adjustment), or they can make a photo look way off (often too yellow). Again, either Color Balance or Variations can help; although you may really need to go to the "Extreme Thing" technique to zero in on the correction needed. Subtle adjustments can be difficult to assess.

Layers: New Possibilities of Control

The key to understanding layers is to realize that they separate your adjustments into distinct and isolated pieces of an image. Think of it as putting a stack of identical photos on your desk. Each photo is a layer in that pile. When you look at the stack from above, you only see the top photo. Cut a piece out of that top photo and you can see some of the photo under it. If you keep cutting pieces out of photos as you go down through the stack, you'll be able to see parts of the lower images. If you do something to the photo under a solid layer with no cutouts, you won't see the effect, as the top photo hides it.

To get started using layers, try Adjustment Layers. This can be very helpful with printing, because it allows you to adjust what a photo looks like without changing the underlying photo. Plus, it allows you to go back later and readjust if you don't like the effect on the print. There actually is nothing in an adjustment layer except instructions. These instructions can be set to affect Brightness/Contrast controls as well as color. And since Adjustment Layers always work from the top layer top down, they affect whatever is underneath them. However, if an Adjustment Layer is removed, the original image remains.

You may also find Duplicate Layers quite helpful for printing. These are layers with identical images in them, like a stack of photos. You can experiment and try different effects on the various layers and compare them fairly easily, because all the layers are right there on your computer desktop. Since duplicate layers are separate, anything you do to one has no effect on the others, and you can compare them quite easily.

One of the best ways to use duplicate layers is to work with different layers for specific parts of a photo, then cut out the unneeded parts on each layer. For example, here you see a landscape photo with "ground" (foreground with plants and soil) and sky (**A**). Each area needs to be adjusted separately, so that the image prints well. You could simply select each area and adjust, but the disadvantage to that is in your ability to balance these areas. As you adjust the sky, you may find the ground needs to be readjusted to balance the tones of the sky. This can be done but is harder when everything is in one piece.

Duplicate the image twice so that you have three layers counting the bottom (the safety layer on the bottom stays unchanged). Consider the layers from top to bottom the same as the photo: sky on top and ground on the bottom. Adjust the sky so it looks good, ignoring what happens to the rest of the scene (**B**). Then remove or cut out everything but the sky and distant mountains in that layer (**C**). You can do this by: using the Eraser Tool; selecting everything but the sky and deleting it (make sure you feather the selection); or using a Layer Mask if your program has that capability.

Do the same thing for the ground layer (**D**), making this part of the image look its best. You don't need to remove the sky part of this layer because the top layer, the sky, is covering up the ground layer's sky. You can make some final tweaks to the image to adjust where each layer has its main effect by removing small segments as needed. You now have a complete image made up of separately adjusted pieces or layers (**E**).

Because layers are separate entities, you can go back and tweak any layer, affecting only that part of the photo, which can be very helpful as you are refining a print.

A

B

C

D

E

Using Layer Masks

Layer Masks are add-ons to layers that control what is actually seen on a layer. They can be extremely valuable in getting the most of an image, yet I know from experience that this is an intimidating part of image adjustment for many photographers. Many who could benefit from this very useful tool never really work with it, but any effort made to learn Layer Masks is time well spent.

While you can erase or delete part of a layer that you don't want, this removes pixels permanently. It can be difficult to put back the pixels if you change your mind. With a Layer Mask, you "mask out" parts of the layer to remove it, but you can restore those parts any time you want by painting into that mask.

Suppose you have a scene that needs some darkening overall, but part of the image, quickly loses detail out no matter what you do with Levels or Curves. The answer is to use an Adjustment Layer to create an overall correct exposure, not worrying about those washed out areas. The Adjustment Layer automatically comes with a Layer Mask—it will show up as a small white box next to the adjustment icon on the layer in the Layers Palette. (**A**) This is active when the Adjustment Layer is created, and you can get back to it at any time by clicking on it.

With the Layer Mask active, you can paint with black to mask the layer, removing the effect from the photograph. Painting white brings it back. Think of it this way. You turn off a light to make a room dark—you can't see it. You turn on the light to brighten it—you can see it. Wherever there is black in the Layer Mask layer, the effect is off; white turns it back on. (**B**) So back to our image—paint black "over" the areas in the layer mask that you don't want affected and the overall adjustment is turned off. It appears as it did before the image was altered, yet the rest of the photo shows the effect of the Adjustment Layer. (**C**)

Knowing this trick lets you tweak individual parts of an image for brightness, contrast, color, and more by using Layer Masks. If you need to fix only a small

A

B

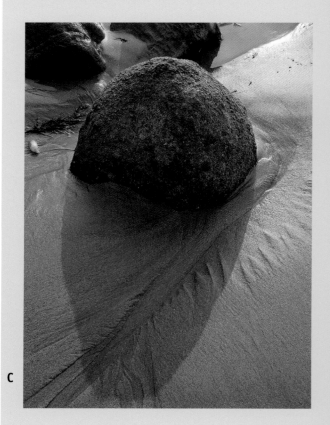

C

part of the image, create an Adjustment Layer, fill it with black (most programs have a Fill command), then paint in the effect with white only over the area actually being changed.

Here are a few things to think about and try as you experiment with layers:

1 **Combine selections with layers**—You can select part of one layer and copy and paste it to a new layer (Photoshop automatically pastes to a new layer). This keeps it separate for adjustments. Making a selection before creating an Adjustment Layer will make a mask that limits adjustments to that selected area.

2 **Rename layers**—As you work, give each layer a distinct name appropriate to it (on the latest versions of Photoshop and Photoshop Elements, you just double-click on the layer name). This will make it easier for you to find and work on a particular layer.

3 **Use the Multiply mode on weak or washed-out images**—Duplicate the image onto a second layer. Then change the layer mode to Multiply. This will intensify the washed out image, often making it print much better.

▶ **The weaker image at top was intensified to create the one at right by adding a layer (either a duplicate or adjustment layer) and setting the layer mode to Multiply.**

The Multiply mode works very well to bring out drama in skies.

4 **Use the Screen mode on dark images (or parts of images)**—Copy a dark photo to a new layer. Now change the layer modes to Screen. You'll often be pleasantly surprised at the detail you can bring out in the dark areas without making it overly gray.

Use Screen mode to brighten dark images and bring out detail.

5 **Use Layer Masks with Multiply and Screen**—It is fairly intuitive to copy the actual image to a new layer and use Multiply or Screen mode. However, you can quickly do the same thing and use less memory. Add an Adjustment Layer without adjusting it (just click OK in the dialogue box without making any adjustment) and then choose Multiply or Screen. Use the Layer Mask to adjust where the effect occurs.

© Pete Turner

Photographer

Pete Turner

Maestro of Color

Pete Turner is considered one of the great masters of color photography. His graphic color compositions have found their way into everything from high-end advertising to books and galleries.

Turner started working with Epson printers a few years ago. He immediately started using them for proofing his work for publications. He has steadily upgraded his units and now uses both desktop and wide-format models. He prefers to use paper with some weight, a matte or luster finish, not glossy, and is always experimenting, looking for papers that best express his graphic color sense. And although he continues to use the printers for proofing images, he now also uses them for making fine art prints for collectors and galleries.

Turner is extremely happy with the quality he gets from his printers. That's a far cry from how he felt working with photo labs, since he was often disappointed in the results. To get around the problems, he developed his own proprietary system for getting the colors he needed, a process that was both tedious and laborious. Now, using Epson printers such as the Stylus Photo 2200 and Stylus Pro 7600, he's been reborn in his passion for experimentation and precision. What's more, he's happy with the longevity of the Epson prints, since his business relies on the prints lasting a long time.

He feels that a digital darkroom that includes Epson printers is a tremendous tool for the photographer. "It's one thing to look at a photo using a monitor, but quite another to sit down with a large print in front of you. You see things more clearly, including things you might otherwise miss. Then you can make the photo better, enhance it, check again and make it even better. An Epson printer gives color photographers a darkroom right in their studio with virtually instantaneous results."

Turner feels that photographers and Epson are on a great path for the future. "Epson is moving at light speed," he says. "These printers are incredible."

Turner's Web site is www.peteturner.com.

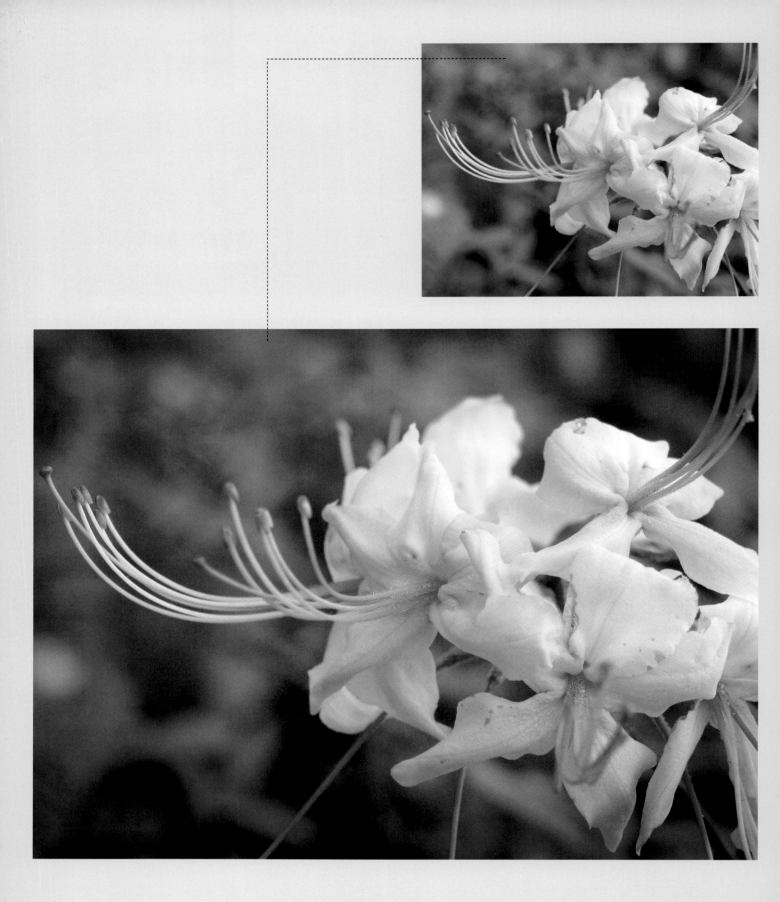

Finishing Touches

What separates a good print from a really great print? There are lots of things, including: paper, printer settings, brightness/contrast, and color adjustments, all of which we've covered. In addition, there are some special finishing touches that you can do to your digital image file that will add that extra something to make your print really shine.

Grain and Noise Management

Grain has been with photography since it began, but became really important when film formats were reduced with the birth of 35mm. Sometimes we find we have too much grain in an image, yet other times we increase grain for creative effect. Either way, grain has a strong impact on how a print looks.

Visually, "noise" in a digital image file is essentially the same as grain. The irregular speckled pattern of either can be distracting and can even destroy a good photograph. Worse, we may inadvertently increase or enhance this grain while working on a photo in the computer.

Here are 10 common places for grain or noise to rear its ugly head in our photographs and ways to reduce it:

1 **Film grain**

A general rule is that higher speed films have more grain than lower speed films (e.g., ISO 400 compared to 100). The grain in film can also be affected by processing. **Solution:** Use fine-grained films whenever you can. The best are those with a film speed in the ISO 100 (or lower) range.

2 **Sensor noise**

Digital camera sensors can generate noise. This happens with all sensors in low light and long exposure situations, though more expensive cameras typically do better in these conditions. In addition, smaller sensors will generate noise because of their size, particularly at higher ISO settings. **Solution:** Use noise reduction techniques for long exposures. Avoid ISO 200 and 400 with compact digital cameras and minimize the use of ISO 800 and above for digital SLRs.

3 **Exposure**

Underexposure causes increased grain in color print films. Digital camera sensors don't like underexposure either and may kick in noise. **Solution:** Be sure the exposure is adequate. This is especially critical in low light and when shooting light, highly reflective, or backlit subjects. Add exposure or use a flash if needed.

4 **Scanning**

Low-priced scanners can be very susceptible to noise, especially in the dark areas of an image. In addition, you'll find differences among even the most expensive scanners in the way they capture film grain. Avoid the really low-priced units, as they tend to pick up a lot of noise in the dark areas of an image. **Solution:** Make a quality scanner a priority item when purchasing your set up.

5 **JPEG artifacts**

Too much compression when saving to a JPEG file, or repeatedly opening and saving a JPEG image, can create little blocky details that look like chunky grain. This is most apparent in same-colored areas with slight gradients of tone such as the sky. **Solution:** Use JPEG (a compression format) sparingly and don't use it as a working format in your image-processing program. Set your camera to its highest quality compression, even though that does mean larger file sizes.

6 Digital artifacts

Sky can be a problem for digital cameras, especially lower-priced cameras or those with fewer pixels. Sky tone varies in a subtle gradient from horizon up. A sensor must make sense of that gradient, yet it can only deal with bits of it at a time (via pixels). This can cause a grain-like pattern in the sky. **Solution:** Realize that subtle gradients may emphasize grain. When sharpening the photo, avoid plain sky areas.

7 Out-of-focus areas

Out-of-focus areas tend to emphasize grain or noise in an image. **Solution:** Remember that out-of-focus areas and large expanses of one tone emphasize grain. If necessary, select the sharp areas and separate them from the rest of the photo before sharpening the image. Never sharpen out-of-focus areas.

8 Image-processing software

Your image-processing software can amplify the appearance of grain or noise. Hue/Saturation, for example, can dramatically bring out undesirable grain/noise effects in the sky. **Solution:** Avoid over-processing of the image.

9 Sharpening

Indiscriminate sharpening and oversharpening can enhance grain and noise to the detriment of a photo. **Solution:** Avoid oversharpening the photo. Sharpen only the sharp parts of your photo.

You will never completely eliminate grain with standard photographic procedures. Sometimes grain can be interesting and can even add to the sharpness of a photo. This is why you can't just blur out grain—it may be needed to keep a photo looking sharp, especially in key areas of the image.

Sharpening the Image

Sharpening has nothing to do with making an out-of-focus or blurry image sharp. What sharpening does is bring out the sharp details in a file. Digital camera files do not gain their maximum sharpness coming directly from the sensor. This is due to a number of factors related to the physics of sensors. The scanning process also does not automatically sharpen the image as it is scanned. Cameras and scanners will often let you do some sharpening at this point, but this might not give the best results.

Usually, you will want to sharpen your file just before printing for three important reasons. First, the appearance of sharpness is affected by image processing, so if you sharpen too soon, you can end up sharpening the wrong amount. Second, sharpening is best done based on a final print size, so you get the best results by adjusting the settings for a specific print size. Third, sharpening too early can adversely affect image artifacts because added processing can then make them look worse.

The tool to use for sharpening is Unsharp Mask. (The name is left over from a process in the commercial printing industry.) This is an extremely flexible tool that includes three controls: Amount, Radius, and Threshold. You will see all sorts of formulas for these settings and most of them work. I will give you some numbers and ways of using the three controls as a good place to start.

Amount is the intensity of the sharpening. It looks for edge contrasts and then increases their difference. I typically use a number between 100 and 200% with Photoshop and Photoshop Elements (other programs often have different ranges—you may have to experiment a little). Look to see how small detail is affected, and watch that you don't oversharpen, making the image look too harsh and edgy. I find that digital camera files often look good around 120–140% and scanned images in the range from 150–200%.

▲ Be careful not to over sharpen a photo (above right).

◀ Use selections as needed to only sharpen what needs to be sharpened in a photo.

◀ Grain is a problem if out-of-focus areas are sharpened too much. Set Threshold higher on Unsharp Mask to reduce grain or noise "sharpening."

◀ Or, you can sharpen only specific, selected parts of a photo.

Radius determines how far the program looks for an edge change in order to make the sharpening effect. Generally, I use a number in the 1–1.5 pixel range (they can be set as decimals), using lower numbers for smaller file sizes (3 megapixels or 10 MB or less) and higher numbers for larger files. Again, watch out that you don't overdo this. It will cause "ringing," white rings at the junctures of contrast changes, and produce a harsh, over-processed look.

Threshold tells the program at what contrast to look for differences along edges. Low settings give the strongest sharpening effect. However, if you have any noise or grain in the image, a low threshold will cause it to be sharpened, making it more visible. Use 0 when noise is not obvious, but a low threshold from 3–6 (up to 10 with severe cases) when noise is obvious, especially with smaller digital cameras. As you increase the threshold, you will usually need to also increase the Amount setting.

If the controls seem intimidating, you can try a handy plug-in from nikMultimedia called nik Sharpener Pro (www.nikmultimedia.com), which uses Unsharp Mask techniques, but hides them behind a user-friendly interface. Sharpener Pro automates some of the process and is designed to optimize sharpness for a particular size of print. It is a Photoshop-compatible plug-in, so it works with many programs that recognize this standard. It uses very understandable sliders, such as paper type and size, to control the sharpness.

Edge Burning

Early in my photographic career, I sat down and read all of the Ansel Adams books on photographic technique. I found a lot of great information. Adams was a superb printer. If you ever get a chance to see one of his photographic prints at a museum, you will see the work of a true master. His books cover the art of printing in detail.

▲ **Edge burning darkens the edges of the photo (as seen in the lower image) before printing. This technique is an easy way to make a print look more dramatic.**

One important factor that Adams stressed was controlling the brightness of the edges of the print. He felt, as have many master black-and-white printers, that the edges should be darkened to keep the eye in the photo. Adams would spend time on most photos burning in (darkening) some or all of the edges to refine his print. Although I have seen some of his prints that had very heavy edge burning, Adams did it so masterfully that most people don't notice this technique.

For "edge burning" our prints, we don't want to use the Burn Tool available on many programs. This is a great tool for tweaking small areas of an image, but the Burn Tool may look blotchy when applied to a large part of the image.

The technique I will describe will give you edge darkening that is never blotchy and is actually easier to do than using the Burn Tool. You simply select the outside of an image and use the Brightness/Contrast control to darken it. Here are the steps:

1 **Select the outside of the photo**
Use a freely moving selection tool such as the Freehand or Polygonal selection tools for most flexibility. For a more automated approach, try the Elliptical tool. Select around your subject, staying a little away from its edge. There is no absolute with this. You have to experiment to see what you like best.

2 **Invert the selection**
Your selection was made around the subject (meaning it is included and the edges excluded). Since you want a selection that includes just the edges, invert the selection (in the Selection Menu).

3 **Feather the edge**
Make a very big feather (or blending) of the edge—at least 70-80 pixels and something over 100 wouldn't be out of line. This will vary depending on the photo, how much blend you like, and the image size (**A**).

4 **Now you have several choices:**
• **Use the Brightness/Contrast control** to darken the selected area—Over adjust it at first so you can see the effect, then bring the control back until it looks natural (**B**). Now, turn the preview on and off and you will be amazed. The undarkened image just doesn't look right!
• **Or use layers**—Copy the selected area to a new layer then adjust Brightness/Contrast for it. This gives you a little more flexibility and control as you can also adjust the layer opacity for effect.

• **Or use adjustment layers**—Use a Brightness/Contrast Adjustment Layer with the selection (which will usually create something called a Layer Mask) to darken the outside of the image.
• **Or use a filled layer**—Again in layers, you can add an empty layer, then fill the outside selected area with black. Change the Layer Mode to Multiply, then bring the Opacity of the layer way down, probably 10-15% (this is highly dependent on the photo).

All of these work. There is no absolute best. You may find you like the ease of one or maybe the control of another. The last effect does have a slightly different look.

A

B

Borderless Prints

Borderless prints from the local minilab have become a standard. You can duplicate this look with any printer by using special borderless papers. These allow you to print over a perforated edge, which is then removed to make a borderless print.

However, a number of Epson printers make this even easier with their BorderFree™ technology that allows you to print edge-to-edge, borderless images without trimming the paper. You can't do this with all papers; your manual (and the Epson Web site) will tell you which papers support borderless printing. You do have to be careful of thin papers, as the ink can over-saturate the edges. Borderless papers and printer capabilities are available from 4 x 6 to 11 x 14 inches.

One really great way to go borderless is by using an Epson printer with roll paper capabilities. You can set up a whole series of photos, such as an entire folder done in FilmFactory, or by queuing up print after print in any program. Then print 4 x 6 inch prints continuously on the roll paper. Some printers even include an automatic cutting feature.

Borderless printing is fairly simple as long as you have the right paper. In Windows, open the printer and select the right paper in the driver, then set the mode to PhotoEnhance or Automatic.

Then click on the Paper tab, select Sheet Feeder as the paper source, then click the No Margins box. Be sure you have the right paper size, too. Then click OK.

For Mac, the process is similar. Select File>Page Setup. In this dialogue box, click on No Margins. Be sure the paper size is correct and Auto Sheet Feeder is selected. Click OK, then go to File>Print, choose the correct paper type, then set the mode to PhotoEnhance or Automatic, and Print!

With roll film printing, obviously this is a little different. You need to be sure Roll Paper is chosen and not Sheet Feeder.

▲ Borderless prints are possible with many Epson printers. You do need to set the printer driver correctly to tell the printer to print that way.

Unique Borders

Special borders can enhance and complement photos that you want to hang on the wall or use in a unique display. I am not talking about the standard white border of a photo, but a unique border applied to the edge of the image file and printed with the photo.

I will cover some simple borders that you can do quickly and easily. With a little practice and some experimentation, you can create even more effects with variations on these techniques. There are also programs available specifically designed to make borders, such as PhotoFrames from Extensis (www.extensis.com).

Black Line and Colored Borders

A very easy border that often enhances a print is a simple black line around the image. This is especially true for light images or photos that have large areas of white near the edge of the frame. In addition, a simple black line border is an effective way to define the area of a photo on a page.

There are many ways of doing this effect. Here are some:

1 **Border command**

Select the entire photo (Ctrl/Cmd A). In the Select Menu of Photoshop and Photoshop Elements there is a Modify command. Under that you'll find Border. Choose that and set a border between 1-4 pixels (this varies with the size of the photo and your taste—small photos need the smaller pixel dimensions). Fill this with black and remove the selection.

◄ **A simple black line can be an easy, yet elegant way to define the edge of a photo.**

2 Outer selection

Use the rectangular selection tool. Make a selection that starts close to, but not at, the upper left corner, then goes close to, but not touching, the upper right, then close to, but not touching, the lower right (the lower left is included automatically). Invert the selection so the outer edge of the photo is selected and fill with black.

3 Stroking the edge

Photoshop and programs like it allow you to "stroke" an edge to add a black border quite nicely. Make duplicate layer of your photo by copying it to a new layer or double-clicking on the background layer of a flattened photo in the layer palette. Then double-click that layer (or go to the Layer menu and find Layer Styles) to get the Layer Styles menu. Select the Stroke option, change the color to black and set the position to inside. You can alter the size of the stroke to fit what looks good to you. Generally, just a few pixels works, but this should be determined by the print size.

Use the same basic techniques to create a colored edge border. This can be very effective if you select a color that is in your photo. You can also use holiday or seasonal colors for an image that might be used in a greeting card. Color effects often look best with a bigger border than what is used for the black line technique. Select a border size (or paintbrush) of 5-10 pixels. The rectangular marquee can also be used to make a wider selection around the outside of the photo.

These techniques do cut into the photo. With a narrow line, as used with the black line technique, this usually doesn't hurt anything. However, with wider colored borders, this can be an issue. In this case, you may need to enlarge the "canvas" of the photo, which will make your photo file larger to allow a border, but will not change the actual size of the image.

In Photoshop and Photoshop Elements, you increase the canvas of the photo under the Canvas command. There you add a little size to the photo (adding pixels or fractions of an inch), keep the photo centered on the canvas, and click OK. This will add a border that is the color of the background. If you do this and the color isn't right, just use your Magic Wand selection tool (the one that selects things based on a single click on the photo) set to a low tolerance. This should select the border area quite well. Then add your color.

Drop Shadows

For a unique and fun photo effect that adds some dimensional qualities to your print, try a drop shadow. Some programs will do this automatically (there are drop shadow layer styles in both Photoshop and Photoshop Elements). However, there is an easy and highly flexible way of doing drop shadows that I like to use. Here are the steps:

1 Add a duplicate layer to your image file (copy your photo to a new layer).

2 Increase the canvas size of your photo to add about an inch, more or less, all around the photo. Experiment and see what you like.

3 Fill the bottom layer with white.

4 Make a rectangular selection around the photo (Ctrl/Cmd click on the layer will do it for several programs).

5 Add a blank layer on top of the layer stack.

6 Fill the selection with black on the new layer on top. You will now see a black rectangle.

7 Deselect.

▲ Drop shadow

8 Move the black rectangle layer down one layer in the layer stack so that it's below the photo layer. This will now be the drop shadow layer and can be named as such. The photo will now appear.

9 Be sure you are on the black rectangle layer, then move it so the black starts to show on the right and lower edge of the photo above. You can actually make this shadow appear on any side, having it on the right and bottom fits a convention that the average viewer can easily relate to. Move it until it seems to create the shadow effect that you like.

10 Blur the drop shadow. Gaussian Blur is the best as it is most controllable. Blur the black box until it looks like a nice shadow edge.

11 Lighten the shadow until it looks good to you by using the Brightness/Contrast control (you don't need any other tools, as there is no range of tones to deal with).

You can use colors for this shadow for special effects or to make a shadow that seems to go better with the photo. Add this color to the selection instead of black. Sometimes a subtle change works well, such as using warm or cool black for the shadow.

Fancier Edge Treatments

The potential for variety and creativity in edge effects is great. I'll give you some ideas that you can take and try, but be careful that the border does not overpower the print. I've seen subtle colors in a photo get lost because of a too-brightly colored border. The bottom line is, go for the simple. Photos tend to be complex enough without overburdening them with overly detailed borders. Now, let's look at a few easy-to-do, simple edge treatments:

1 **Painted On**
Take a hard-edged paintbrush with white as the color, and then paint the edge of the photo with an irregular, almost jerky, movement, always staying at the edge. This will make a unique, one-of-a-kind edge that will sometimes look great. Be sure you save the image as a copy first, so you apply the effect to the copy. Experiment with different sizes and types of brushes for varied effects.

▲ Painted-on edge with drop shadow.

▲ You can use a photo as an edge treatment for an image by putting a larger background photo on a layer under your main image.

2 Painted on layer

You can do the same effect as in 1 with more flexibility by using an empty layer over the photo. Paint the edge treatment in that layer. You can then go back and change the edge treatment in the layer. In addition, you can add effects to this edge treatment by experimenting with the choices in the Filters or Effects part of the program's menu and applying them to the edge layer.

3 Photo-in-edge

This technique actually uses another photo-graphic image (often a texture) as the edge of the photo. A very nice way to get this edge photo is to use a flatbed scanner to actually scan something, such as the pattern of leaves, fabric, or any photograph of a texture or pattern. You start with the textural edge photo as the base. Then you copy your main photo and paste it in as a layer over the texture. You could also paste it into a selection that was in the right spot. Size the main photo so that the textural background shows up as a nice border. The amount of border you decide to show will depend on its texture and what looks best with the photo. A black-line border, or a drop shadow, can add to the overall effect. Ideas: A flower photo with a border of leaves, a birthday party with an edge of balloons, a seascape with a border made from a close-up of the rocks along the shore.

◄ Soft edge

4 Soft edge

This is a very romantic photographic treatment that often looks good with portraits. You can do this in a couple of ways. Make a rectangular selection around the outside of the photo, just inside from the edge. Feather this at least 20 pixels (the larger the image size, the larger the feather needed, so with a big feather, you get a softer edge). Then invert this selection and fill it with white. With layers, you can fill this selection on a new layer, which will give you more flexibility, since you don't actually change the underlying photo. Experiment with the amount of feathering as this can radically change the effect.

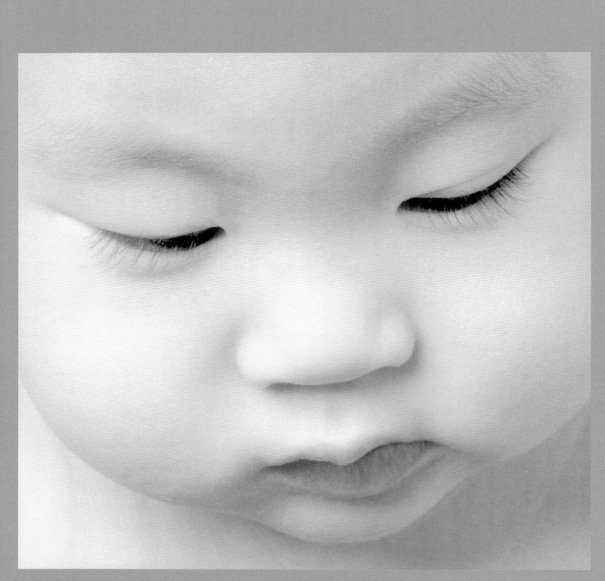

© Jack Reznicki

Jack Reznicki

Commercial Photographer

Many people have asked why I love my Epson printers so much. Is it the rich colors, the control over my imagery, the long-lasting inks, the hot-looking machines? Nope. There's something else I love about Epson photo printers. As a commercial photographer, my imagery may get me the jobs—but the prints from my Epson close the deals. Before Epson prints, I used to make my own C-Prints for my portfolio, or I would hire some of the best C-printers in New York. Compared to either of these, Epson's prints sing a richer tune with a deeper and richer palate of colors. My portfolio books a higher percentage of jobs since I switched to Epson prints. Art Directors just react better to the richer colors and the depth of the prints. Plus, I can shoot something one day and have it in my portfolio the next day—looking exactly the way I want it to look. More often than not, fast turn around and greater ability to get what I want out of an image makes the difference in getting the job.

The first time this happened was a few weeks after I got my first Epson printer. I got a call from an agency looking for baby images for an upcoming campaign. I submitted a portfolio that included two new images. They were close-ups of the faces of an Asian and an African-American baby. Both shots were extreme close-ups; both babies were looking down and they were tightly cropped, cutting into the babies' foreheads. The African-American baby looked great, but the Asian baby just melted on the page. I was able to get the baby's skin to be so light and airy that it was almost translucent. With the African-American baby's delicate features on the opposite page, it was a portfolio spread that made you stop and look—it blew away the Art Director and the client. They decided to do a whole campaign based on that look. I knew I had a lot of good images in my portfolio, but it was those Epson prints of the babies that nailed the job for me. I'm positive of that. The campaign for baby immunization ended up on posters all over New York. How cool is that?

A few months later I was up for another big campaign for a national hotel chain. They were looking at a lot of photographers. A lot. Finally, it became a choice between me and one other photographer. The art buyer called and said it would come down to our black-and-white portfolios. Could I send my black-and-white portfolio for the next-day delivery? I replied that I my black and white portfolio was out. Would two days from now be OK? The art buyer reluctantly said OK, but no later, since they had to make a decision.

Well, not only was my black-and-white portfolio "out", it was also non-existent! I spent the day converting color images into black and white using Photoshop. When I printed the images, not only did they print quickly—they looked smashing! Photos like these would have each taken 2 to 3 hours in a conventional darkroom. Not to mention all the extra effects I could do digitally, like adding grain to make some of the images look a little more "rough." I knew that this client wanted a candid, from-the-hip look. I overnighted the new, still warm, portfolio and kept my fingers crossed. Two weeks later I was on a plane with my assistant getting ready to shoot a great new hotel campaign. Thanks, Epson.

Sometimes it's that last 5% that makes the difference between getting an assignment or not. I know in my heart that without my Epson printers, it's likely I would not have landed these two campaigns. Even now, the prints still blow me away! The control, the ease and speed, the color—these should be more than enough reason to fall in love with these printers. But for me, the "closer" is the jobs I can point to and say: "The Epson prints are what landed these deals for me."

Dialing in the Print

Getting the best print you can is obviously a key concern of most photographers. All of the things covered so far in this book affect this goal, from the types of inks to the paper used. But it is important to remember that this is not something new to digital. Frankly, traditional color printing done in a darkroom was often very difficult to control. This is one reason why Ansel Adams never did much color printing and preferred black-and-white. He said that color prints always looked to him like a television slightly out of tune.

This chapter is designed to help you "dial in the print," to make it something that you are pleased with and proud of. I am not going to give you a heavy-duty color management discussion, although I will cover this topic. I want to give the average photographer practical, down-to-earth ideas and tools for getting better prints. Some ideas, such as monitor calibration, are critical parts of the process for every one. Other concepts, such as printer/paper profiles, may or may not be appropriate for your printing needs.

The tools of color management can be basic to quite advanced. Advanced tools are more expensive, may require more work and will complicate the process. They absolutely help the photographer who either needs them or feels more comfortable when he or she has the most control over the process. That control isn't for everyone. It fits a way of working, a style of using the computer and photography that is perfect for some folks, but annoying and uncomfortable for others.

Color management of any type, whether automated at the printer driver level or advanced control used by the printing industry, is designed to help all the different devices used for digital photography talk to each other in a similar language. Scanners see colors differently than digital cameras, monitors read colors differently than printers print them out. Computers and associated devices see photos similarly based on color management built into the technology, but they differ a bit like people talking in different dialects of the same language.

Color management allows dissimilar digital devices, from scanners to monitors to printers, to communicate in such a way that color remains fairly consistent on all of them. I say "fairly" consistent, because these devices can deal with color in very different ways. For example, a digital camera may record a series of colors that emphasizes certain ones over the others in a different way than a particular printer and paper portray that same series.

I believe that if color management is taken to extremes, it can be distracting. The photographer's purpose should be to make a great print, not necessarily match an arbitrary original image, which may or may not be accurate to the scene or the photographer's intent.

If I can help photographers relax and have fun making prints, rather than getting uptight from pressures to do things "the right way," I know they will enjoy printing more. Printing your own photos should be fun and not a technical test!

The Difference Between the Monitor and the Print

A key to dialing in that great print is to understand that the monitor image and the printed image can never look identical. The print is viewed with light reflecting off its surface, while the monitor shows us an image based on transmitted light of glowing red, green, and blue phosphors. Reflected light and transmitted light can never look identical to our eyes. So, we will aim for as close a resemblance as possible.

However, and this is very important, your monitor must be calibrated. Calibration is not done to make the screen look just like your prints. You calibrate your monitor so that you have a neutral and predictable workspace. You want to know that when you make changes on the monitor to an image that you are changing the image in predictable ways so you can get better prints. Calibration tools and software are very simple and easy to use. They all use a special sensor that sits on the screen and reads a set of carefully controlled tones and colors from the software. The software then analyzes this and creates a monitor profile that defines how it displays colors.

You can find excellent calibration tools from ColorVision (www.colorvision.com), Monaco Systems (www.monacosys.com), and Gretag (www.greytag-macbeth.com).

That said, it is worth considering if a print should even try to match what you see on the screen. You look at that photo on screen in a very specific environment that might not be anything like where the photo will be displayed. In addition, looking at a print is a very different experience than viewing a photo on a monitor. So how do you know if you have a good print? Do you like it or not? The bottom line is always about the print satisfying you, by itself, in the environment that it is most likely to be viewed.

You need to evaluate your prints in the conditions you expect to display them in. Bright rooms vs. dim hallways, daylight vs. incandescent—these factors can change the way a print looks. You may want to make a small print for reference (it is faster to print and correct) until you know the right settings, then make corrections for your big image based on that.

Color Space Setting

Visible color range

Epson Stylus Photo series

sRGB Color Space

◀ Computers define color in a range of hues called a color space. Digital cameras typically use the sRGB color space. Epson printers can handle more than that, making their P.I.M. system quite effective in getting the most from digital camera images.

Epson PRINT Image Matching

In order to get better photographic-quality prints from digital camera files when printed on Epson Stylus Photo printers, Epson developed a new technology called PRINT Image Matching or P.I.M. It was created as a way of making digital cameras and printers work together to produce photographs that "print truer-to-life than ever before."

Well, most photographers know that real life is never the same as a photo and "true-to-life" is always very subjective. You might think of P.I.M. as an automated color management technology that controls the way digital cameras "talk" to a printer so that they really do work together to optimize the image in the print. What it does is attach information to the digital camera file at the time of image capture, information that can help make a better print, such as camera features used (e.g., flash or white balance), exposure modes and so forth.

What happens is that a digital camera then "remembers" certain information about the photo

as it is taken. For example, a close-up shot could be remembered as such so that the printer software would receive instructions on emphasizing detail and sharpness. If the camera has modes, a Portrait mode image might be recognized as needing attention for flesh tones.

Many digital camera manufacturers are including this technology in their cameras to allow them to quickly benefit from Epson printing equipment. EXIF (Exchangeable Image Format) data is an international standard that imbeds camera data into the digital image file and actually is based on the P.I.M. concept. However, P.I.M. actually includes more information for printing in this imbedded data.

This is a somewhat automated way of printing, but it is very useful for those quick snapshots that everyone needs to print at times. Once you start refining your image for printing as described in earlier chapters, this is no longer an important tool. If you do want to use it, check your printer manual for instructions.

Quick Guide to Color Management

I consider printing a craft, not a simple science that guarantees consistent results if one just follows the "rules" of color management. Color management is an evolving part of computer science. But printing is as much an art as it is a science. Two photographers may print the same image quite differently. Ansel Adams used to talk about how his prints in the later years of his career were often a different interpretation of the negative compared to earlier prints. I am a firm believer in treating any photo printing as a craft and not a "computer thing."

Here is a quick overview of things to think about when dealing with color printing in the digital darkroom. I'll cover some of these in more detail afterward.

▲ **Calibrating your monitor is the first step in color management. A colorimeter and software are required.**

1 Monitor calibration

If you want the best prints, you must calibrate your monitor. Calibration is critical to give you a neutral and predictable workspace on your monitor so that you can make consistent and predictable changes to your images for better prints. Calibration tools and software are quite affordable and easy to use.

2 LCD vs. CRT

In the future, we may all use LCD monitors. Currently, however, they have several problems that make them less than ideal for critical photographic work in spite of their "cool factor" and small size. They can be hard to calibrate properly, they have angle-of-view issues (which change how colors and tones are seen), and they do not have the best tonal range. Some LCD units overcome these problems, but they are quite expensive. You can get top-of-the-line CRT monitors with the highest calibration capabilities for half the price of even the lowest-cost, acceptable LCD units. A cheap LCD will make printing harder.

3 Paper

Paper is different. Perfectly printed images will look different on different papers. You have to find the best paper for your images and work within its capabilities.

4 Printer driver

We looked a bit at the printer driver earlier in the book. It definitely affects how color is managed when making the actual print. It is the "translator" that takes the data from your computer and sends it to the printer. Be sure you set it right and check for updates at Epson's website.

▲ **Epson's printer driver allows you to set the paper type.**

5 Test

In the traditional darkroom, it is standard procedure to test and adjust to get the best images. No matter what techniques and workflow you use, testing and adjustment is just as important with digital printing. If an archer doesn't hit the target because conditions for the day are different, he or she would not complain about the conditions, but simply adjust for the wind and other variables. We can do the same with the computer. Essentially, this is what printer and paper "profiling" is all about, and we have a number of ways to deal with this.

Testing

At any level of printing, you always need to do some sort of testing. You need to know how a printer works, how papers react to the ink, how a subject looks on paper, and so forth. Every craft requires you to try something, evaluate it, and then make adjustments based on what you have learned. Profiling a printer is a more involved way of testing, though luckily, this has been done for you by Epson in the printer driver, and in addition, there are specific profiles on Epson's website for photographers who need them.

Still, no matter how much you use all the technology available, you need to fine tune any print so that it best meets your needs for the image, and the only way to do that is to make a print and look at it. Is it a good print for you? Is it a satisfying interpretation of the photograph that stands on its own? Anyone who looks at that print will only be seeing the print. They won't ask you to transport them to the original scene; they won't want to see what was on the LCD of your digital camera; they will only see that print.

But sometimes you will run into an image that just won't cooperate or maybe you are trying out a new paper—either way, you want a quick testing method that doesn't waste a lot of time, ink, and pages. Plus, it would be good to test systematically as you make adjustments. I have had images fool me. I would think I needed to tweak color one way to get a more satisfying print, but by using a test system, I discovered I was off. I slapped my head and said, "No wonder this didn't print right!"

I am going to give you a way to make a smart test print that works for me and has worked for photographers who have read this book or attended my seminars. I am going to describe the process using Photoshop and Photoshop Elements. Variations of this technique can be used with any image processing program—you simply need a way to create a series of images on a page.

Here are the steps when using Photoshop and Photoshop Elements:

1 Open your photo and go to Picture Package (this is under the File menu, under Automate in Photoshop and Print Layouts in Photoshop Elements). You will now see your photo displayed as multiples on a page.

2 Be sure the page is set to a printable size, typically 8 x 10 inches at 240 dpi.

3 Select a print layout that has the same size photos and an amount between four and nine. Four gives you bigger photos to review, nine offers more variations. You can choose Flatten All Layers or not (you gain some flexibility by keeping the layers, but this technique does not require it).

4 Hit OK and let the program work its magic. You will get a page of photos. Rotate the page orientation if needed.

5 Leave the upper left photo alone and consider it your control, an unaltered representation of the image on the monitor.

6 In Photoshop, select the image to the right of the control photo with the rectangular selection tool. Make an adjustment to it and record your adjustment. You can alter color, exposure, or both, depending on what you are trying to test.

7 Select the next image in the sequence, make another adjustment, and record that, too.

8 Do this for all the small photos. At first, your adjustments may be random. But after some experience, you'll make adjustments in more methodical ways because you'll be better able to read your photos for printing.

9 Print this new page out and look at all the small images. Which one looks best, or at least heads in the right direction towards best?.

You may have to make another print with some additional adjustments to refine the image. You will, however, begin to discover what corrections you need to make in order to get the best color and exposure for your image and the paper.

You can make your own test print by creating an image with multiple copies of your photo, then adjusting them individually for a single print.

Control   Darker   Lighter

Increasing Red >

Increasing Yellow (decreasing blue) >

Adjustments

Based on your testing, you will learn what corrections to make. You can then adjust your printing file so that the image prints better. It is always a good idea to create a printing file that is sized and sharpened specifically for the print you need. Then the changes and adjustments never affect your master file.

Method 1: Adjustment Layers

This is my preferred way of making adjustments for printing as it is not destructive to the original file and is transferable to other images. You simply add an Adjustment Layer to your photo for each separate correction you need to make: Levels, Color Balance, Hue/Saturation, etc. A real advantage is that if your adjustment isn't quite right, you can simply alter the Adjustment Layer settings to change the effect and even reset the controls without affecting the pixels of the underlying image. Since these layers are just instructions, they can also be dragged and dropped onto any open photo in the image-processing software. This allows you to make an adjustment on one photo and drag that identical change to another.

You can even make a special correction file that holds Adjustment Layers for specific types of images and papers to use repeatedly. Add whatever Adjustment Layers you need to correct the original photo. Next, resize the photo to 4 x 6 inches at 100 dpi (this is only a viewing file) and do a "Save As" and give it a name related to the subject and paper you are using, such as LandscapeLuster. Whenever you print this subject type on this paper, just open the file, and drag and drop the Adjustment Layers onto the new photo. You have instantly corrected your photo for printing, yet you have not changed the base image at all, plus you can easily tweak this photo by changing the Adjustment Layer controls.

◄ Be cautious when making image adjustments directly to the photo because you are changing actual pixels.

▲ Adjustment layers are always safe because they let you make adjustments without changing pixels.

► Since Adjustment Layers are not size specific, you can make a special correction file that holds Adjustment Layers for later use.

▶ Print adjustments can also be made directly with the Epson printer driver. These can be saved for repeated use.

Method 2: Printer driver

Epson includes the ability to make printing adjustments in their printer drivers. In the Advanced Settings on the driver, there is a color correction window. This includes sliders that control the brightness/contrast and color settings we covered in earlier chapters. These controls adjust the printer output without affecting the image file itself.

The Epson driver settings include the self-explanatory Brightness, Contrast, and Saturation controls. The color correction controls, however, only mention Cyan, Magenta, and Yellow, but not all of us think in terms of adding and subtracting just these colors. It will help if you remember that Cyan is always paired with Red, Magenta with Green, and Yellow with Blue, so adding any color will subtract from its opposite part of the pair. Conversely, subtracting any color will add to the complementary color. Once you have these printer adjustments dialed in, you can save them for future printing with a particular paper.

Method 3: Adjusting the image directly

For simple changes, you can apply adjustments directly to your photo just before you print. You need to be cautious when doing this because you are "changing pixels" and you could lose your refined image if you save over it. You should keep a master copy—an unadjusted version of your final image. If you print on different paper, for example, you can make corrections from a standard image, not one that changes with every print.

Advanced Color Management

What we have just been doing is color management of a sort, managing the colors of your image. However, the term color management has some specific connotations concerning photography and computers. Color management is a way of making different digital imaging devices, from scanners to printers, work together to create colors that they all "understand."

Color management tools are like using a detailed map to get to a destination. However, if the destination in the first place is incorrect, no map in the world will make it any better. If I have a great map to a desert hotel and my family hates the desert but loves mountains, I will probably be better off heading in the direction of the mountains in the distance, even if I don't have a map. Color management is no different. It can give you a print that meets all the "right" criteria based on the "map," but if the print does not express your intent, then the destination is wrong.

There are several basic concepts you need to understand here: color space, device profiles, and workflow. There are many good references that go into these in far more detail than we can deal with here. I want to give you enough information to understand what these concepts are all about and how they fit into a color management model.

Adobe RGB (1998)   **sRBG**

Color Space

Color is a highly variable thing. People can look at the same color and call it different things. The computer has to break down all the colors of the world into digital data that can be later reconstructed in a way that recalls those colors. To do that, the computer requires some parameters, so computer engineers have defined color as a space that can be calculated, interpreted, and controlled.

Color space is not a single entity. There are basic, overriding spaces like RGB (red, green, blue—the standard computer space) and CMYK (cyan, magenta, yellow, black—common to the commercial printing process). RGB is a larger color space than CMYK, which means a wider range (or gamut) of color is possible in an RGB device than with CMYK output. Please note that while ink jet printer ink is based on the CMYK set of colors, the printer actually works best with RGB data.

The two main variations of the RGB space are sRGB and Adobe RGB (1998)—check your image processing software for Color Settings to find these. You will see them as choices on digital cameras and in the color space option of image-processing programs. I have talked with Epson engineers and they assure me that their printers will print just fine from either space. I can also tell you from experience that the printers can make great prints from either color space.

So what's the big deal about these two spaces? Adobe RGB is, in a sense, a slightly bigger container than sRGB; it encompasses a wider range of colors. This may or may not be an advantage. Most digital cameras really produce a set of colors closer to sRGB than Adobe RGB, regardless of which setting is used. The result is that when an image with Adobe RGB is brought into the computer, the colors may seem a little duller than the same image in sRGB. Since there is a bit more color range in Adobe RGB, you have more to work with to get the colors you want. But you also have more work to do!

Using sRGB or Adobe RGB is as much a workflow issue as it is a question of what colors do you really need. I have found that many photographers like sRGB better because it lets them get to an image they like faster. Photographers who like to spend more time adjusting an image may find Adobe RGB better. Commercial photographers generally use Adobe RGB because they have very specific needs for color adjustments related to the products they photograph. For most of my shooting, I don't need that range and like what I get with sRGB, so I frequently use it. For a photographer who wants a file that always has the most information, that wouldn't be appropriate. The bottom line is that both color spaces can produce great photos for prints—different perhaps, but not arbitrarily better or worse. Some of the images in this book started in sRGB, some in Adobe RGB (they all end up as CMYK for the printing press). I can't honestly say that either color space was a consistent advantage for these photos.

The point is to find a color space that works best for your way of working, then stick to it. A photographer that works steadily in either one will get to know it and how the colors respond. The way to truly get great prints is to know your materials and what they can do for you.

Device Profiles

A profile is a characterization of a device's color-rendering capabilities. We use device profiles in color management to allow different imaging devices to communicate about color in the same way. Profiles come from a standard image that is measured for each device. Computer hardware and software manufacturers have standard test images that they use. Calibration software will include such images as well.

When you calibrate your monitor, you are creating a profile. The measuring device and software look at how the monitor displays standard colors, then build a profile for that monitor. There is also software for custom profiling of other devices as well.

For a large majority of photographers, the profiles built into their equipment will work well. Monitors should be calibrated with specific calibration devices so specific profiles are created, however. Epson supplies excellent profiles for its printers and papers. Choose the paper and print quality settings carefully, and the printer driver's algorithms usually do a wonderful job. It is the results that count, not the specific steps you use to get there. If the automatic settings work for you, then use them. They simplify the process.

In programs like Photoshop and Photoshop Elements, you will see the profiles come up when you open the Print with Preview dialogue box. If Show More Options is checked, you will see a section with choices for color management. For many photographers, the Print Space Profile default Same As Source will give excellent results. (Check that the Source Space uses the same color space you are using.)

However, you can also change profiles at this point. In the Print Space Profile dropdown menu you will see a whole set of profiles appear. Choose the one that is appropriate to your printer and paper type. When you choose a profile, you will also find a new set of menu choices called Intent. There is a slight difference between Perceptual and Relative Colorimetric (ignore the other choices). Although both work well, you may find that one works better for you. Keep Use Black Point Compensation checked.

If you set the profile this way, then you need to make a change to the Epson printer driver when it appears. Go to Advanced Settings, then find ICM and check it. You will now see a choice about ICC Profile; click on No Color Adjustment because Photoshop is doing the adjusting.

In the end, the goal of all this is to get an equipment setup that renders color in a predictable way. Color management is about consistency from input to output, allowing all devices to communicate, so that they understand each other's use of color. This allows you to focus on the results and not the mechanics. Then color management becomes simply another tool for the photographer to use to support his or her vision.

Simplified Color Management

It all comes together in this way:

1 Calibrate your monitor using monitor calibration tools and software.

2 Set your color space to either sRGB or Adobe RGB (1998). Since most small digital cameras (including digital SLRs) are based on sRGB, you may find sRGB is good one for you. Adobe RGB (1998) gives more flexibility with certain colors.

3 For printing, choose color management with either Print Space "Same as source" or use a specific printer/paper profile.

4 Be sure your printer driver is set correctly.

5 Test and refine your image to get prints that you like using the tools described in this chapter.

© Graham Nash

© Graham Nash

© Graham Nash

Photographer

Nash Editions

Digital Fine Art Printmakers

In the days when digital imaging was a novelty, rock star **Graham Nash** of Crosby, Stills & Nash fame and his tour manager Mac Holbert were looking for a way to print Nash's digital black and white photographs. When they were introduced to an ink jet printer designed for the pre-press market, they knew they had to have one because they saw the potential for using it to print art. Little did they know at the time that they were co-founding the world's first digital fine art printmaking studio. Today, Nash Editions is arguably the leader in the field, having devoted more than a decade to mastering the fine art digital printing process.

Stunning image quality and permanence are critical to the work of Nash and Holbert. The first ink jet printer they owned gave them quality output but was difficult to keep running properly because it was designed for proofing and not photography. Today they rely on Epson's photo and pro graphics ink jet printers, which deliver image quality and permanence with minimal maintenance.

"The ease of working with the Epson printers is key to us," Holbert says. "It's amazing to be able to walk into the studio in the morning, press a button for three seconds, and within two minutes, the printer is ready to start printing astonishing, photo-quality output."

Even more important than reliability is the wide color gamut, exquisite detail, and longevity that Epson's newest archival printers give Nash and Holbert. "The Epson printers capture exquisite details that you just can't get with traditional techniques," Holbert says. "You know the moment in the darkroom when you watch an image slowly emerge in the developer tray—it's magic. Well, you get the same magic with Epson printers." Furthermore, because the printmakers are often asked to print on alternate substrates, Epson's versatile paper handling is also a big plus for Nash Editions.

Nash and Holbert maintain Epson is the leader in digital photography because they listen and respond to photographers and artists like them.

"Epson didn't ridicule us," Holbert said. "They recognized the capabilities of our business and our pioneering spirit. They were interested in our problems and in pushing the future of printing."

Nash Editions' Web site is www.nasheditions.com.

Displaying the Print

Once you've made a nice print, you can do many things with it. In this chapter, I'm going to give you some ideas on displaying photos. There are whole books devoted to this, so I just hope to inspire and encourage you to try out some of them. Have fun with your prints!

When you want a great photo for a framed print on the wall, your Epson printer can create it. But, if all you want to do is put a photo on the refrigerator, that's okay, too. Making a new print is so easy compared to the old days of finding a negative or slide, then going down to the local lab and ordering an enlargement (and waiting days for it to come, then having to get it reprinted when it wasn't right).

Tack-Up Display

The refrigerator is always an honored place for a photo! Kids, parents, and grandparents consider this a great place for photos. There are lots of places that prints can be tacked up, from a dorm room bulletin board to the walls of a workspace cubicle.

Obviously, you can throw any photo up and tack it in place. The print doesn't have to be fancy. However, there are some things you can do to enhance this display and show off your photo and subject (the latter is often most important!). Here are some ideas:

1 **Size**
   Big photos always make an impression, but these display areas don't always have lots of room. 5 x 7 inch sizes can be ideal—you can even print two of these on a single page.

2 **Contrast**
   Because these areas don't always have the best light and there is a lot of visual competition, photos often need a boost in contrast and color saturation to make them standout.

3 **Borders**
   Borders, especially simple lines, can add a great touch to photos used in tacked-up displays.

4 **Words**
   Try adding some simple text, maybe the names of the people in the photo or a location, either in a corner of the photo or below it.

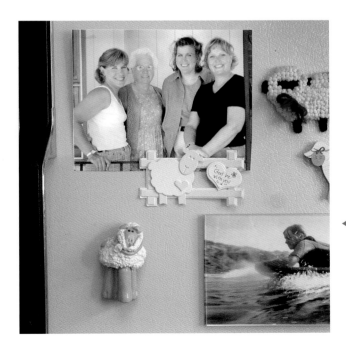

◄ **Because you can make prints easily with your printer, you are free to create them for everything from a formal wall display to the refrigerator.**

Sometimes simple, direct frames are the most effective way of displaying your images.

Simple Frames

The next level of display is to get your prints into a frame of some sort. Framing sets off the print and protects it from the environment. It gives an impression of importance to the photo.

I think that some photographers don't frame their photos because it just seems like too much trouble, finding the right size frame, matting and mounting the photo, and so forth. While a matted photo can be a stunning use of your images, this is not a necessity for having a nice print display on the wall. Try these simple ideas:

1 **Quick frames**

At craft or art-supply stores, you can usually find an assortment of frames that you simply pop open, put your photo in and then snap the glass back in place. Use your image-processing software to make an exact-sized print (including any border or edge treatments) to fit the frame size. The Original Format Frame by MCS Industries is one that I've found very useful because you can buy it in an 8 1/2 x 11 inch size that allows you to use a print directly from the printer without doing any trimming. I like to use these frames with prints that do not print to the edge so I can add an edge-treatment or have a nice border that sets them off.

2 **Fome-Cor™**

Made of a rigid foam between two sheets of heavy paper, Fome-Cor™ is that ever-adaptable art supply material. It is a very light, yet strong, display material that comes in a variety of thicknesses. A very easy display can be made by mounting your photo to a piece of Fome-Cor™ then cutting it out so that you have a rigid, borderless photo that can be attached to a wall (this is a common photo display for tradeshows). You can use spray-on adhesives (use them outside or in a well-ventilated area and protect the surrounding areas from spray drift) or special mounting sheets made for the purpose. Many copy stores will do this for a small fee.

3 **Poster frames**

Craft and art-supply stores also often have inexpensive poster frames that can be used for quick framing of prints. These frames use clear-plastic rather than glass over the image, then have strips of flexible molding that cover the edges and hold the plastic, print and backing together. These can be an inexpensive, easy-to-use solution for larger prints. You can cut them to fit a specific size by using a very sharp knife (cut through the plastic slowly, using moderate pressure over multiple passes of the blade, so you don't crack the plastic).

Albums

Photo albums are great. We all love to take a look at photos from over the years. But they can be a chore to put together, so many old prints sit in shoeboxes at the back of a closet.

Rather than trying to put every photo into an album, try making theme albums of larger prints. The whole phenomenon of scrapbooking takes this idea to new and creative heights. Check out any of the excellent scrapbooking books on the market for ideas. Craft supply stores will even have whole sections devoted to this.

Themes are a great way of using albums. Print a set of images from a trip or an event, such as a birthday or other party, and put them all in one album. Use extra pages for text to explain what the photos are all about. Don't try to fill the album—just remove unneeded pages so that the album seems complete.

Or, you may simply want to put your photos together in a nice album without the work of fancy scrapbooking. How ever you use albums, look for acid-free paper and mounting sheets. The plastic pages should be labeled as "archival" to assure they will protect the photos and won't cause any deterioration.

▶ **Of course, you'll want prints for an album of family memories and history.**

© Jan Press Photomedia, Livingston, NJ

© Jan Press Photomedia, Livingston, NJ

© Jan Press Photomedia, Livingston, NJ

Advanced Mounting and Framing

You can customize your print display with all sorts of mounting and framing techniques. You can have these done for you at a framing shop, or do it yourself from materials purchased at craft and art-supply stores. This can be quite involved, with a lot of special tools and techniques. That's beyond the scope of this book, but here are some ideas to keep in mind while looking to custom display your prints:

1 **Match your frame to the display area**
Look for frames that fit and complement or supplement the setting. A room with antiques begs for a frame and matte with detail and a feeling of age, so a silver metal frame is likely to look out of place. On the other hand, a rough wood frame won't look at home in a modern office with fabric and metal details.

2 **Black frames are always safe**
Some people might consider black frames boring, but actually that's why they are perfect for photos. They don't compete with the image, nor will they conflict with any colors. Black usually makes colors look better. You can never go wrong with a simple black frame.

3 **Make your print the star**
Sometimes art supply and framing stores will try to sell you an elaborate frame and matte. You want your photo to be the center of attention, not the frame. Be sure the detail and color of a frame and accompanying matte make your photo the star.

4 **Use size to set off your image**
Sometimes a big photo in a big frame is the most dramatic way to use your photo. In this case, you often want a minimal matte treatment because the photo will actually look bigger if it is pushing the edges of the frame. Another effective display technique is to place a small

▲ **Frames come in so many styles. You can often find one that fits the setting and tone of your display space.**

photo in a larger frame, matted in white or a neutral tone. You might use a 5 x 7 inch print in a 16 x 20 frame, for example.

5 **Choose matte colors carefully**
Over the years, I have had the privilege of judging many photo contests. One thing that I have seen as a consistent problem in display contests is a matte color that takes over the photo. An example of this would be a nice photo of pink flowers surrounded by a strong pink matte. I know that a lot of interior designers like such an approach because it makes for bold color in a room. However, it destroys the photo. It takes the eye away from the colors of the image rather than complementing them. You can pick up colors from the print in the matte, but use colors that do not compete with the dominant subject color. Neutral tones can be very effective ways of working with a matte, or use neutral colors with a hint of image colors.

6 **Use acid-free mounting papers and tapes**
Acids in cheap papers and mounting tapes or glues can ruin a print in a few years. Keep your framed image looking good by using acid free materials.

▶ Simple matte colors can range from white to a soft color based on a subtle color in the photo. These are good choices to complement the photograph.

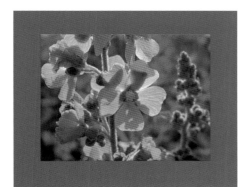

▲ This matte dominates the photograph. Be careful to choose colors that will make your print the "star."

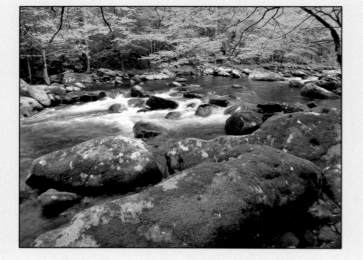

There are many options for matting a photo. All can be effective in the right location. Photos usually look best when the matte is slightly wider at the bottom.

If the borders on the matte are too thin, (top right) a borderless print, without a matte, would probably be a better choice.

Where to Display

Once you've put together a nice presentation of your print, consider how you can best display it. A little planning can dramatically enhance the effect.

Consider your wall space and picture size. A large photo in a small area will often appear cramped, while a small photo in a very big space will tend to look lost. If you can't make big prints for the latter situation, try putting groups of photos in the area. Groupings can be an excellent use of a large area. Theme groupings can add impact to the images, such as a group of family photos or a selection of flowers.

Use whatever size frames work for you, but you'll find it easier to deal with the images both in terms of frames and groupings, if you limit the sizes to a few in any given display area. A hodgepodge of frames might be okay for grandma's stairwell display of the grandkids, but it tends to draw attention to the frames and away from the photos.

Contrast a large photo with several small ones. Or try a group of moderate-sized images in a formal pattern. Photos can be arranged formally (all lined up along at least one edge) or informally (arranged without any edges lining up). It always looks odd to see one photo out of line in a formal arrangement, or one photo lined up with another in what should be an informal grouping. Be consistent so that the group is either informal or formal.

Photos can be chosen to dominate a space or blend in with the décor. The subject and composition of the photo, the size of the print, as well as the type of frame will heavily influence how dominant a photo is on the wall.

Lighting

Your prints will look their best with the right lighting. There are a variety of things you can consider about the lighting conditions to make your prints look a little better.

In areas with a lot of glare, use glare-reducing glass. Some people will use this type of glass all the time, but it can reduce the contrast of a print. This reduces the full impact of Epson photo blacks, which

◀ **Prints look their best in light that favors them.**

are so rich and deep. Matte-finish papers can be another good way of dealing with glare.

Recognize that direct sun as well as bright fluorescent lights can cause fading in prints. Be sure prints displayed under these conditions are made with archival techniques (described in more detail in Chapter 14 on long-lived prints). You can also use special UV-filtering glass to help.

If you can't control the light in an area, you may need to control the print. A dark print may have a beautiful mood, but it is likely to just look muddy in a dark hallway. Choose a brighter image for such a location or make the print brighter.

Dedicated light for prints can be a great idea for areas that include prints as an important part of the décor and when you have special prints that deserve the best light. Avoid fluorescent lights in these conditions. Standard fluorescents never make any photo look its best. If you must have fluorescent lights, try some of the daylight-balanced models.

Avoid glare-producing lights. This is highly dependent on the height of the lights and is one reason why many people use top lighting that carefully illuminates the photo (or group of photos).

Track lighting is ideal for illuminating photos. The light can be directed, yet is above the photos so no glare appears. Low lights can be a problem, because they often reflect in the prints or glass over them. Floor-mounted lights can give a dramatic effect, but they can also give a weird feeling to the frames, because we are not used to this type of low-angled light. Incandescent lights work well, including the soft halogen types often used in track lights. Keep the lights a little away from the wall so the photo isn't lit directly from the top, but not so far away that you start seeing the lights reflected in the glass.

© John Shaw

© John Shaw

John Shaw

Nature Photographer

Considered to be one of the modern masters of nature photography, **John Shaw's** work has appeared in everything from *American Photographer* to *National Geographic* to *Smithsonian*. He is also known as a lecturer, a leader of photographic safaris, and an author. His book entitled *The Nature Photographer's Complete Guide to Professional Field Techniques* is considered a classic.

Shaw embraces digital technology in his work, and teaches seminars on the digital darkroom, using his prints to illustrate what can be done at home with a computer, Photoshop, and an Epson printer. He uses some of the latest Epson models, including the wide-format printers, to make prints of his images that have been scanned from 35mm and 6 x 17 film. As for the papers he prefers to use, he likes the look of Epson's Premium Luster, but likes canvas and fine art papers as well.

Shaw's business has been strongly affected by his use of Epson printers. He says that before Epson he intentionally stayed away from selling prints. "I was always disappointed with prints from a lab," he says, "no matter how 'professional' the lab billed itself." Now Shaw can produce prints exactly the way he wants them to look. In addition, he can do this on his own timeframe—no back and forth to a lab. Consequently, selling prints has become a great addition to his stock photo business.

The biggest secret to getting the most from the printers? "Calibrate, calibrate, calibrate with a monitor calibration tool." With this tip he says he can make prints of different sizes or different papers, and they will all match in color. "Try doing that in an analog darkroom!"

With the introduction of Epson's latest printers, he feels the traditional darkroom is, for all practical purposes, dead in the water. "Combine these printers with powerful but affordable computers running Photoshop, and suddenly pro lab quality is available to anyone."

Shaw's Web site is at www.johnshawphoto.com.

© John Shaw

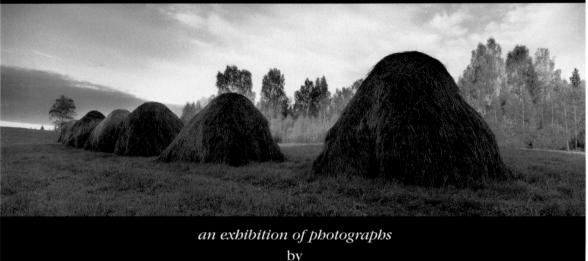

Latvia
the green heart of the Baltic States

an exhibition of photographs
by
Niall Benvie

MONTROSE MUSEUM, PANMURE PLACE, 13TH JULY - 9TH AUGUST 2002

Printing Projects

Making a great print can be very satisfying. In addition, all the techniques you learn in producing a print you like can be applied to lots of different printing projects that include photos in interesting ways. This can range from a simple "For Sale" poster to an elaborate brochure. Being able to use photos in many different ways, both for pleasure and business, is a real joy for photographers.

I am going to give you a variety of ideas with some tips on how you might do them. Try them out as they interest you. Experiment with different applications of these ideas. For example, a flyer featuring your photos could show off your images to a magazine. You could use exactly the same technique to feature photos of collectibles, antiques, jewelry, and more. The neat thing about the computer is that you can experiment without any real cost. If you don't like something, you delete it. And if you do like it, you can print as many copies as you want!

Postcards

Postcards are such a wonderful way of using your photos and sharing them with others. Postcards are so quick and easy that you can use them for many things: birthday greetings, birth announcements, thank you notes, business promotions, or keeping in touch. Here are a few ideas:

1 Make them a standard size that allow you to either print on small sheets (such as, 4 x 6 inches) or four on an 8 1/2 x 11 inch page so you can print more efficiently. All Epson printers will handle 4 x 6 inch paper directly, which do individual cards as you need them.

2 Fill the card with the photo. Use borderless settings with printers that offer them. You can also buy special postcard papers that allow you to print past perforations that you remove to get a borderless image on printers without borderless capabilities.

3 Use text on or near the photo. Postcards are often put up on refrigerators, bulletin boards, and so on. If the reason for the card is not included on its face (in text), it can lose some of its effect. For business purposes, always include your name, phone number, and email on the photo side of the card. You want your recipient to be able to associate you and your business with the photo. Whatever the purpose of the card, keep the text simple (e.g., Happy Birthday, Sammi or ACS Natural Designs), bold and in an easy-to-read typeface and size. Use colors that complement the photo (white or black are safe).

4 Create a special design for the back. You can design it like a standard postcard with information about the photo plus room for the address and a message, or you can be as creative as you like—you just need a space for the address and postage. Make sure that it fits the format of the photo and paper. You can get paper that can be printed on both sides: one side is the photo, the other the text. Personally, I like using adhesive printing paper, because you can peel it off the backing then stick it to your photo. It gives the photo a little more substance as a postcard.

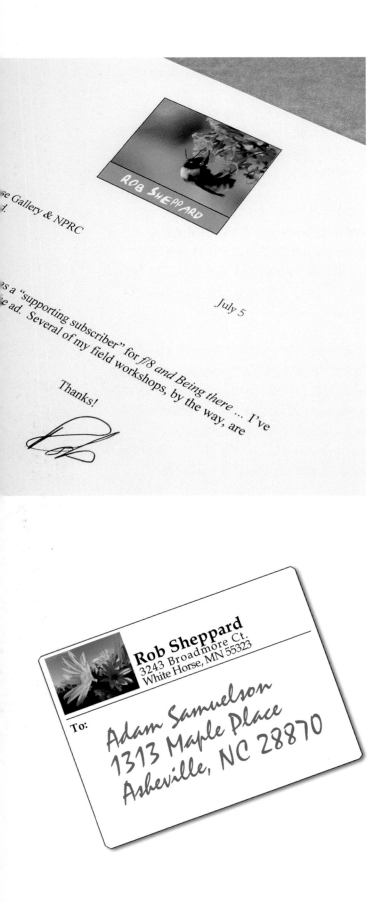

Letterhead

A business friend of mine incorporates a small photo in his letterhead and he changes it every time he sends me a letter. This is a very impressive, yet subtle, way of reminding people what he is doing in his business.

I started adding a single photo to my business letters a few years ago. It really dresses them up. Of course, photography is my business, but it is fun to share people, places, and things that I have photographed. In addition, I made up a simple letterhead that incorporates a photo.

Most word-processing programs can add photos (see below). Many low-end photo and design programs actually include letterhead designs that you can modify with your own work. The advantage of doing a letterhead or adding a photo to a page in a word-processing program is that you can save a master that you can use for typing the letter itself. You can, however, print out letterheads designed in other programs that you can run through your printer again later to print the letter itself.

You should reduce the size of your photo so it is the size used on the page at the needed image printing resolution, such as, 2 x 3 at 300 dpi. When working in programs like Microsoft Word, add your photo into a text frame, don't add the photo directly to the page. By inserting a text frame first, then inserting a photo into it, you can more easily move and position the photo on the page.

Mailing Labels

Mailing and address labels are so easy to do today that I am sometimes surprised that I don't see more of them used with photos. You can get labels of almost any size, plus many photo and design software programs include specific templates for the exact label you buy. Not all of the labels use photo-quality paper (though many do) but I'm not sure that's really all that important. Having a nice photo on a label is so unique that it will stand out no matter what label paper is used.

There is not a lot involved with labels except that the image and text (such as your return address) have to fit. I like to print a quick check print using cheap paper to be sure the labels are lined up properly for the label paper. Hold it in front of a piece of label paper then up in front of a light to see if it all fits.

You should think a little differently about choosing a photo for a label than if you were making a big print. Photos on labels are small and they need to be understandable to work right. Many great photos don't look that great when reduced to fit the small size. Try to pick photos of single subjects without a lot of small detail. You will need to resize your photo in an image-processing program so that it fits this size at a printing resolution (such as, 1 x 2 inches at 300 dpi). If you use a large image size, say an 8 x 10 at 300 dpi, without reducing it, you will end up with a very large file that could slow down your computer and even make it crash. Do a Save As once you've resized your photo so your bigger file is protected and you have a small file just for this purpose.

Photo Montage

When you put several photos on a single printed page, you gain some wonderful opportunities to make a very special print. One way of doing this is to create a montage. This technique layers photos on and around each other so that the group of photos becomes one unit. It can be a great way of expressing something about a subject that cannot be done in a single image. Think about starting with a portrait of a child, then adding images of him or her playing soccer. Or how about a portrait of two senior members of your family along with photos of them through their many years.

The easiest way to make a successful montage is to plan it around a single strong photo. There are certainly other possibilities, but when you use a single strong photo as the largest image, it becomes

a foundation for the montage as well as an anchor for the viewer's eye. Then build the image with smaller photos that interrelate with the big one. Montages are usually best made with either a design program or an image-processing program with layers, as either type of software allows you to move the individual elements around by simply clicking and dragging the photo. You will want to do a lot of moving of the montage pieces around until it looks just right.

Two opposite, but very effective, refinements to a montage are drop shadows and blended edges. Drop shadows added to the individual photos really make them stand out and give the overall image some interesting depth. Play around with the softness and opacity of the drop shadows. Blended edges allow you to link and combine photos in some very striking ways. Create a soft edge (the technique is described in the border section of chapter 8) to start and try using either a soft-edge eraser, or a layer mask, to better blend photos.

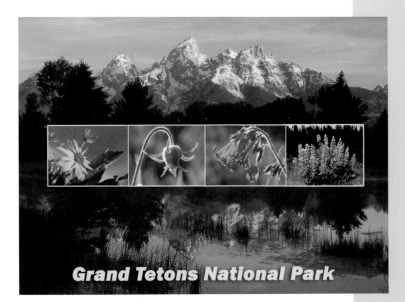

Grand Tetons National Park

▲ By combining several photos together in a single montage, you can make a very special print.

Printing Multiple Photos on a Page

There are many situations where you want or need to print more than one picture on a single sheet of paper. You may want to print out a whole group of 4 x 6 inch photos onto sheets of 8 ½ x 11 inch pages, or maybe you want a "picture package" that includes several different sizes on a page. Either way, it can be more efficient and cost effective to maximize the use of the paper.

You have a number of options for doing this. Adobe Photoshop and Photoshop Elements include something called "Picture Package" in the File menu under Automate or Print Layouts. You can select a whole series of multiple-picture-on-a-page layouts that can be printed with duplicates of the same photo or different images. The program does the processing of the images for the layout automatically. A number of other image-processing programs do this as well, including Microsoft Picture It! (www.pictureit.com).

In addition, there are some stand-alone programs that make multi-picture printing very efficient and don't require you to open an image-processing program. These include ArcSoft Photo Printer (www.arcsoft.com) and ACDSystems FotoSlate (www.acdsystems.com).

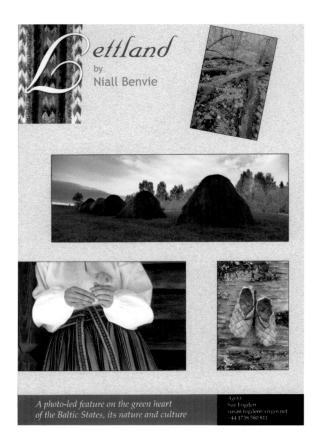

▲ **Flyers that combine text and photos often make a strong statement. They can easily printed on an Epson printer.**

Photo Flyer

A flyer is like a montage because it has multiple photos on a page. You could certainly build a montage for a flyer. The difference is in the use of text and purpose. A flyer is something that has a strong message, often business related, so the photos and text must be carefully chosen so that they work to support it.

Flyers are often weakened by poor use of text and by the use of too many small photos. You may want to try out some of the design templates offered in many low-end image-processing programs and design software. Use them as a starting place and modify to your needs. Check out the design books by Robin Williams for some excellent ideas for building a flyer and other designed projects.

◀ **Printing multiple pictures on a page is a more efficient use of your printer and your printing paper.**

Here are some tips to make your flyer work better for you:

1 Use clean, easily read text

No matter how great a message you have, if the reader finds your text hard to deal with and won't read it, you've wasted a flyer. The simple typefaces such as Helvetica, Arial, Times Roman, Garamond, and Eras are not exciting but are very readable. Anyway, your photos should be the center of attention for the piece, not a fancy typeface. You can use fancier typefaces for short text like a headline.

2 Keep typefaces to a minimum

Too often, I think, because there are so many typeface choices in the font menu, flyers become a mishmash of type that is confusing to the reader.

3 Pick a key photo to be your star

Make one photo a focal point by keeping it large and dominant on the page. This gets far more attention from the reader than many small photos.

4 Use small photos to support the big one

Small photos add context and depth to your message, and they visually support the big photo as well. They make it more dominant from the contrast.

5 Pay attention to details

It is easy to look at the bold, attractive photos on your page and miss important details. It is a good idea to print out the page for this reason—I have often missed things on the computer screen that looked obvious when printed out. Watch out for missing text or pieces of text—this happens when you move things around on the page and the elements interact with each other. Be sure photos line up when they are supposed to. If two photos look like they are in a row, but one edge is a little off, it makes the design look sloppy.

6 Use edge borders

A thin black line around photos can really help set them off on the page.

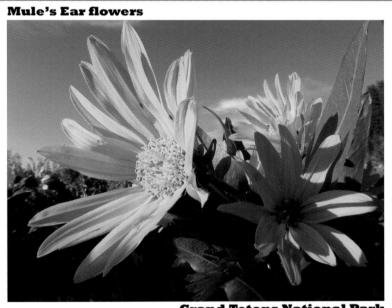

▲ When used with photos, text needs to be easy to read and carefully placed, whether on a straight print or in a brochure.

Newsletters

Family newsletters with photos have become very popular in recent years, in part due to the computer and ink jet printer. They are now used more often, not just at Christmas. In addition, many businesses have found newsletters to be a great way to keep in touch with clients and customers.

Because newsletters are fairly easy to produce, they too often look like they have been thrown together with little thought to the design and use of text and photos. Many design and low-end image-processing programs include newsletter templates that can be excellent starting places (and can be worth the price of the software alone). Broderbund even has a PrintShop program just on Newsletters and Brochures. The Robin Williams books can also be most helpful.

Many of the ideas in the flyer section are just as important for making a good newsletter. A clean, readable typeface is absolutely vital for the main text and should stay the same throughout the newsletter. Any time you change the text font, be sure it is for a very specific reason, such as highlighting a special achievement of someone.

Bold, simple headlines are also important so your reader can quickly understand the newsletter and so that it looks inviting.

Use a few photos boldly and don't try to cram too many images on a page. If they look cramped and fight each other for space, there are too many photos. Look at the front page of a newspaper. Photos are chosen carefully for how they support the stories and gain reader attention. You do want people to read your carefully prepared newsletter. One way to do that is to make it compelling and inviting through the use of selected, but intriguing or engaging photos. Be bold! Feature your photos!

Newsletters have a very specific look. Part of this is a very structured appearance, which includes the location of the title and logo, how the columns and photos line up, etc. Paying attention to these details can make the newsletter more inviting to your reader. And be sure your name, address, and email are included somewhere (in a small box near the end is always good.) It also helps to include some reference in the logo area, so your readers have a reason to remember you.

◀ **Newsletters, a great use of your printer and photos, can communicate to many audiences.**

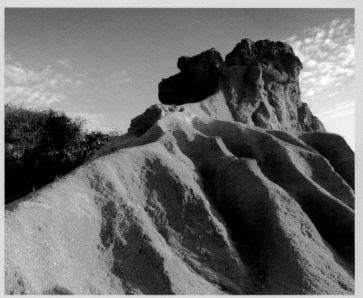

© Joseph R. Meehan

Posters

With the larger Epson printers, both desktop and graphics ink jets, you can make some wonderful posters that can be used for everything from a dorm room to church events to business promotion. This can be a great way to promote organizations you support and use your photography as well.

Putting together a poster is like making a postcard or flyer, but much bigger. All of the ideas presented in those sections can help with posters. Be sure you use a heavy-enough paper for the use (a church poster in a hallway is going to be more stressed than one in an office cubicle).

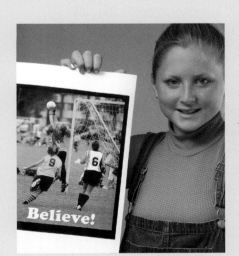

◀ **Posters made with larger Epson printers are often most dramatic if the text is simple and bold.**

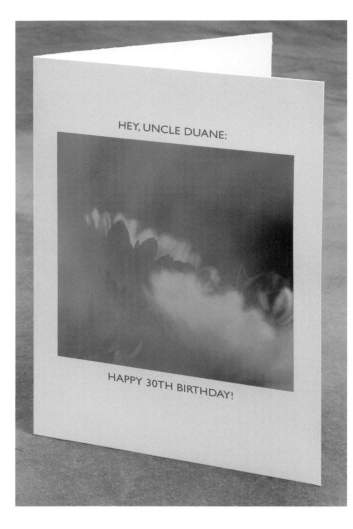

Greeting Cards

Whether it's a grandmother who gets a birthday card with a photo of her grandson saying "Happy Birthday, Grandma," the family friend who gets a thank-you card showing the sender with the gift, or the client who gets a "keep in touch" card with pretty landscape photos personally shot by the sender, each is surprised and pleased to get a unique, personal card that says the sender really cares.

You can get special card papers (and envelopes) that are prescored for borderless cards and for easier folding. They usually include instructions on how to make a card that has text on the inside as well as photos on the outside. Sizing can be a little tricky, so make prints on inexpensive paper first, fold them up to see that everything fits properly. Then hold them up against the good paper to see if everything is printing the way you want. Remember that

standard glossy photo papers do not always fold well. You may find the matte finish papers work better for you.

Many inexpensive image-processing programs include templates for making cards. If you do a lot of cards, they can be well worth their low cost, even if you do higher-end imaging work in Photoshop. Epson has instructions on making greeting cards on their Web site in the Print Lab and Craft Projects section.

Brochures

A brochure can be an excellent way to use your photos in a community organization or a business. The key is planning. I find it very helpful to take a sheet of paper, fold it into the brochure form, and doodle notes and pictures on it. Or, find a commercial brochure you like and use this as inspiration.

I will even print out small photos that I can cut out and tape into place to get an idea of how the photos might look. Admittedly you can do this in the computer, however, a brochure is made to be seen in the hand, not splayed out on a computer monitor, so I want to get a feel for this.

A brochure always has a cover. You need to pay special attention to it, using bold but limited type and a strong photo to get your viewer's interest. Give them a reason to pick up the brochure and open it.

Then you need to look at each piece of the brochure as it opens. Be careful that you don't cram too much text or two many photos into it. That can make it very uninviting, making your reader stop reading and put it down, something that you don't want. Use the tips from the flyer and newsletter sections above about using photos and text. Don't be afraid to use some color for attention, but restrain your use of color to only a limited selection of hues.

Look for brochure templates in many design programs.

Booklets

I have done booklets with many photos as programs and yearbooks for my kids' sports teams, as well as church directories. A full-color booklet can be a very dramatic and effective way of showing off your subject, such as the kids on a team, and is usually received with pleasant surprise even in today's world of computers and high-quality ink jet printers. I once did a 36-page program/yearbook for my son's baseball team and printed all 150 copies on my ink jet printers! Such booklets will definitely take some time to print, but I have found them worth doing because they are satisfying for everyone involved.

Here are some tips:

1 Choose the right paper
A thicker, high white ink jet paper is ideal. This lets you print on both sides and you'll have minimal bleedthrough (photos or text that show through to the other side). I've found that you need a minimum of a thick 24 pound paper or a regular 30-38 pound paper to work.

2 Design a graphic cover
Do something simple with a big title and a big photo. Again, there are many templates available for this in software programs. Avoid having too many photos and too much text.

3 Create a real book
While you might not need a table of contents, it helps to make up one for planning purposes. This will help you include things like an introduction, "chapters" (on specific topics), and so forth.

4 Use a simple font for the text
This makes it inviting and readable.

5 Use photos for contrast
Try some big photos on pages as well as pages with many small pictures. This can make the booklet more interesting.

6 Use moderate photo-quality settings
Unless you are going for a photo book quality and are using the highest quality paper (which you can do), use the Fine 360 dpi or Photo 720 dpi settings (test them with your paper to see which looks better—you can also try some different paper settings in the driver as well). This will give excellent quality while offering faster printing speeds.

Black-and-White and Panoramic Prints

Photography actually got started with black-and-white outdoor images and the tradition of black-and-white landscape work is especially rich. It includes the Western frontier photography of Timothy O'Sullivan and William Henry Jackson, through the grandeur of Ansel Adams, to John Sexton's glowing black-and-whites of today. It was actually the black-and-white prints of Jackson over a hundred years ago that helped influence Congress to set aside the Yellowstone area as the first national park.

A fine black-and-white print can be a wonderful thing to behold, often much better than anything you will see printed in a book or magazine. Yet, getting a good black-and-white print wasn't always easy. The local minilab rarely gave top black-and-white results and building a darkroom wasn't an option for most people.

Luckily, ink jet printers are capable of making superb black-and-white images. In addition, the computer lets us do things to a black-and-white image with more control and precision than you could do in the traditional darkroom.

Getting to Black and White

Most black-and-white photography has been shot with black-and-white film. This is still a viable and challenging way to photograph. Many excellent black-and-white films are available, including the superb "chromogenic" films such as Ilford's XP-2 and Kodak Black & White +400. These are color technology-based films that yield a black-and-white negative, but can be processed at any color minilab in the standard C-41 color print film developers (which makes them very easy to use, even if you don't have a darkroom).

If you shoot black-and-white negatives, you can scan them directly with any film scanner or flatbed with appropriate transparency adapter and enough resolution. You have to tell the scanner you are scanning a negative. If your scanner doesn't let you do a black-and-white negative, just scan it as a color negative and remove the color in your image-processing program.

You can also shoot black-and-white directly with many digital cameras. These give you an image file without color and you can see the black-and-white effect on your LCD monitor.

Many photographers are discovering that the computer provides a new option—shoot in color, then convert to black-and-white. These new-thinking photographers gain some unique advantages that are unavailable when the original image is captured in black-and-white. These advantages are related to filter effects, how different colored filters change the tonality of a scene as it is captured from real-world color to black-and-white.

You can actually make superior black-and-white prints by shooting in color first!

Here's why you might want to shoot color for black-and-white prints:

1 Filtration after the fact

Filters strongly affect contrast in black-and-white photography. Dramatic skies are created using red filters, bright foliage is enhanced with green filters, and so on. You can always filter the color image in the computer, after shooting, to translate the scene into these preferred black-and-white tones.

2 Interactive filtration

Suppose you are new to black-and-white photography and don't totally understand filters and their effects. With the digital darkroom, you can try different filter effects on the same scene and instantly see how they change it.

3 Totally variable filtration

No matter how many filters you take with you into the field, you still have a limited set of filter colors to use in order to control the tones of the scene. In the computer, you can fine-tune the filter colors to very subtly adjust grays in the black-and-white image.

4 Multiple, yet separate filtration

Think of a scene with red flowers against green foliage in a landscape that includes beautiful clouds in a blue sky. A red filter will make the sky darkly dramatic, setting off the clouds, but maybe you don't like its effect on the plants because the red flowers will be light against dark foliage. You could use a green filter to make the leaves light and the flowers dark, but the sky will not be so dramatic. In the computer, you can select the flowers and foliage part of the photo and apply a green filter, then select the sky and apply a red filter effect.

Translating Color into Black and White

There are a variety of ways of translating color images into black-and-white in the digital darkroom: the computer, an image-processing program, and the printer. I am going to explain seven ways of making the color translation to black-and-white tones.

1 nik Color Efex

This Photoshop-type plug-in offers a superb black-and-white conversion tool (most programs, not just Photoshop, can use Photoshop-type plug-ins). It is available in the Color Efex Pro! complete collection as well as the Color Efex Pro! Design Bundle (www.nikmultimedia.com). What makes this little program so effective is that you control the filtration of the scene with a simple slider that goes across a spectrum of colors. As you adjust the slider, you can watch how the colors affect the gray tones in the image. It is like having an infinite set of color filters for black-and-white. In addition, you can control the strength and brightness of the effect as well—try that with a traditional black-and-white filter!

2 Color channels

Photoshop and other advanced programs include the ability to look at and separate the individual color channels that make up an image (usually RGB—red, green, and blue). In effect, this gives you three very different conversions to black-and-white, as if you shot the scene separately with red, green and blue filters. Once you find a color channel that looks good to you, you can delete the others or change the photo into a Grayscale image, which gets rid of all color information. The Split Channels command will separate the color photo into three separate black-and-white images based on the channels.

RGB color

Green channel

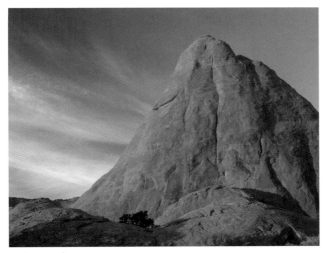

Many imaging programs have a command that will break a color image into black-and-white images based on its separate color channels.

Each channel creates a black-and-white conversion with a distinctly different look.

Grayscale

Red channel

Blue channel

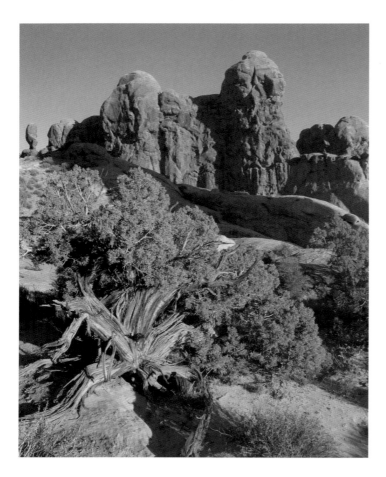

3 Channel mixer

Photoshop has an interesting tool in the Image/Adjust menu called the Channel Mixer. If you open this and set it to black-and-white, you can adjust the tonalities of the black-and-white conversion by playing with the red, green, and blue channel sliders. More of any channel will make colors related to that channel lighter, and opposite colors on the color wheel, darker (e.g., more of red will make reds lighter and blues darker). If the numbers for each channel add up to 100, the photo stays at about the same brightness as the original color image. If they go higher, the black-and-white version gets lighter; if lower, it gets darker.

4 Selections

You can always make a selection to isolate part of the photo before making your black-and-white translation. This allows you to selectively change colors to gray tones, as if you shot part of the scene with one color filter and another part of the scene with an entirely different filter.

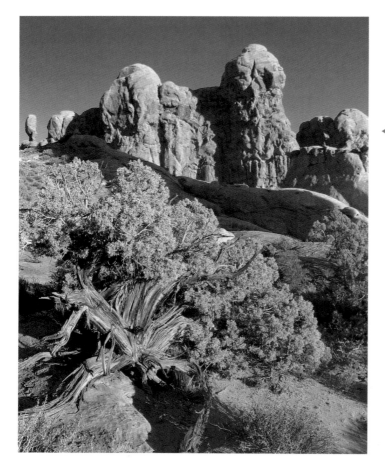

◀ By selecting parts of a photo, you can change them to black-and-white separately and differently. The top photo is a straight grayscale conversion. The lower photo favored red for the conversion in the top and green in the bottom of the photo.

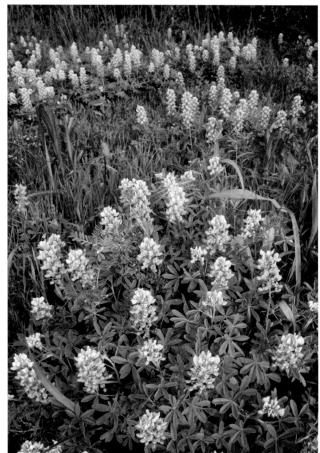

5 Grayscale or Desaturate

Many image-processing programs will let you turn a color image into black-and-white by changing the color mode to Grayscale (which discards all color information), or by using a Desaturate command (which gives a black-and-white image in color). These are quick and easy ways of dealing with images that don't need a lot of adjustment, but on many photos, they may tend to make the image look too gray without enough contrast.

▶

Both the Grayscale and Desaturate commands adjust the tones in a black-and-white conversion in a standard, consistent way that may not give the best results (top right). The bottom photo used nik Color Efex to better control how colors translate into black-and-white tones.

6 Grayscale vs. RGB color for black-and-white

A Grayscale image is a photo without color except black, white, and gray. It is a smaller file than a color image. All of the above techniques can be converted to Grayscale if needed. Having a black-and-white photo in RGB color allows you to color or tone the image with a sepia or cool selenium tone, or other color toner effect.

7 Hue changes

If your program doesn't accept plug-ins and it won't separate channels, you can still make some changes to a photo that will affect the black-and-white tonalities. Use the Hue/Saturation control and change the hues (colors) of the photo before you make the Desaturate or Grayscale change. Change the colors and you alter the resulting grays.

Black-and-White Adjustments

Once you have a black-and-white image, you can continue to make adjustments in your image-processing program. Try increasing the contrast to make the photo more dramatic. You could use Brightness/Contrast for overall effects, but Levels and Curves offer more control. With Levels, bring the left (black) slider to the right and move the other sliders left to increase contrast. With Curves, make the line steeper for more contrast.

You can also dodge (lighten) and burn (darken) parts of the photo as well as darken all the edges (as described in Chapter 8), clone, and so forth, just as you would with any photo.

Black-and-White Image Printing

Black-and-white prints can be beautiful from an ink jet printer. However, they are sometimes hard to print as a "pure" black-and-white photo with four- and six-color printers. Frequently, there will be a slight color tone, even when printing from a grayscale image without color.

Yet, you will get your best results printing black-and-white images as if they were full-color in the ink jet, because that is the only way an ink jet printer will render the full range of gray tonalities. Ansel Adams processed his photos with a toner (sepia for a warm look or selenium for a cool look). So, giving your images tones to make them print better on your printer is really a time-honored artistic technique.

If you absolutely must have only black-and-white tones, there are several options. Epson's seven-color photo printers add a gray ink (which Epson calls "light black") to the normal six colors. It allows these printers to gain more neutral black, whites, and grays while maintaining the range of tones.

You can also check out some specialized black-and-white inks (that replace the colored inks in Epson printers) available from InkJet Mall (www.inkjetmall.com) and Luminos (www.lumijet.com). I've seen some stunning black-and-white prints from these inks, but you do need to dedicate a printer to black-and-white printing in order to use them. This is because you risk clogging the printer head if you switch back and forth from black-and-white printing to color. Note that Epson's printer head warranty doesn't cover damage caused by third party inks.

Regardless of the type of black-and-white printing, you'll often find that the black-and-white photo looks its best with a thin, black border around it. This adds a very classy touch to the photo and makes it look more "artistic."

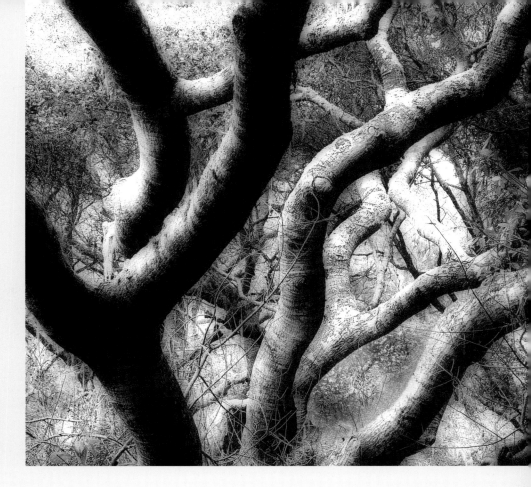

▲ **If a black-and-white image is still in the RGB color space, it can be easily color toned with tools like Color Balance.**

▶ A color tone can add an elegant touch to a black-and-white photo and make it print better on an ink jet printer.

Toning the Photo

If Ansel Adams could do it, why can't you and I? Adding a slight color tone to an image will give it more depth when printed as well as making it easier to print with four- and six-color printers. The easiest way to do this is to start with your black-and-white image in the RGB color space. You then use several techniques to add color:

1 Color Balance

Adjust the color balance to add yellow and red, for warm sepia tones, or cyan and blue, for cool selenium tones, to the photo. Experiment with the amount of adjustment as you make prints, then once you have a good print, record the adjustments for future printing.

2 Hue/Saturation

Use the colorize feature and change the hue setting to give you the color you want. Tone it down with the saturation control.

3 Color layers

Add an empty layer over your photo. Fill it with a blue or warm tone (e.g., yellow-orange), then change the layer mode to color. Tone down the effect by reducing the layer opacity (10-15% often works well).

4 Duotone effects

Change your image to Grayscale, then click on Duotone, if your program has it. You now select the type of tonality you want (e.g., duotone, tritone, etc.). You will see several "Ink" colors, starting with black. Click on the ink and choose a warm color to go with black for a sepia-tone effect or play around with colors for all sorts of effects. Then vary how each "ink" is used in the photo by clicking on the Curves box and changing the curve. There is a live update as you do this, so play until you get exactly what you like. This control allows you to mix colors in some rather unique ways. Personally, I like the first three effects best because they are more intuitive and easier to use.

© Joseph R. Meehan

▲ **Panoramic photos are a great way to use an Epson printer because they can easily give you the proportions needed up to 44-inches long and more.**

Panoramic Photos

Wide-format, or panoramic, photos have long been popular with photographers. Yet, they were often hard to get made into large prints, and the specialized cameras needed for quality pans were expensive and scarce. Photographers have long tried taking multiple pictures of a scene, then lining up and pasting the prints together as a makeshift panoramic, but they could not blend the images together into one. The computer changes this dramatically. Anyone with a camera, film or digital, can now produce panoramic images.

Epson was the first printer company to offer ink jets that could print the long images that panoramic photos required. You can easily print photos up to the full width of the paper and 44 inches long (for standard printers) and with no length limit for the graphics printers. Panoramic images have gained popularity, because Epson printers have been available to print them.

Still, this doesn't mean any subject can be made into a panoramic. You need to compose for and shoot a composition that uses the entire image area effectively. Watch each side and the middle, as there should be compositional elements of interest throughout.

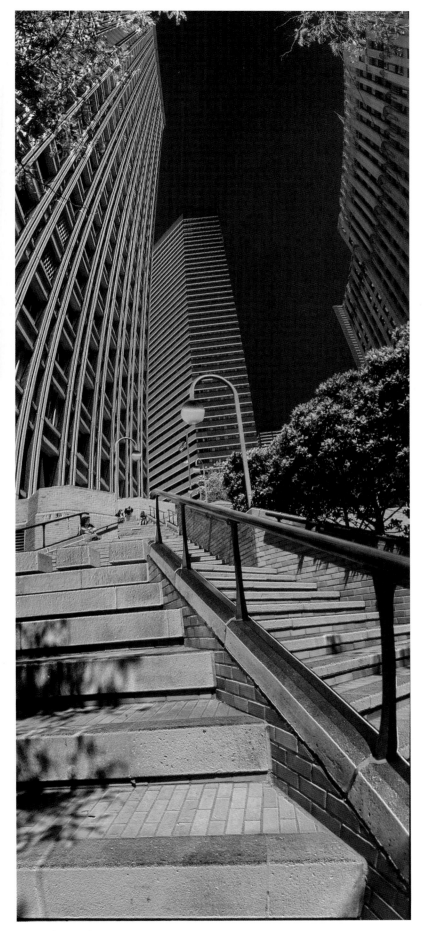

© Joseph R. Meehan

Shooting for Panoramics

To make a good panoramic print, you need to start with the right materials. You could shoot with a panoramic camera and scan the resulting negative or transparency. It will be too big for most film scanners, so you'll need to use something like a high-resolution flatbed scanner with transparency adapter, such as the Epson Perfection 2450 Photo scanner.

Many photographers are building panoramics from images shot with a standard 35mm or digital camera. To do this, you shoot a series of photos from one side of the scene to the other, overlapping each shot, and put them together in the computer. One advantage to this is that you can use the equipment you already have.

◀ **Panoramic images can be more than horizontal landscapes, too. The key to their composition is to be sure there is something interesting from side-to-side or top-to-bottom.**

Even a standard Epson desktop printer can produce a big panoramic print.

Here are some tips:

1 Plan out the panoramic

Figure out what the composition will include from right to left (or top to bottom if you are shooting a tall panoramic image). A panoramic needs to have interesting things happening from one side to another, with no dead space, to keep your viewer's attention.

2 Level your tripod and your camera

As you move across the scene taking photos the camera needs to move in a horizontal plane or the resulting images will be hard to line up. Do the leveling in two steps: tripod first, then camera. You will find everything lines up better if you use a tripod.

3 Overlap the images by 20-50%

More overlap can make it easier to line up the photos in the computer, especially with automated programs, but this also means you have to take more photos.

4 Shoot on manual

Your exposure needs to be optimized and limited to one setting through the entire sequence of images or the final pieces of the pan will be hard to match up.

5 Practice

There is no question that panoramic photography gets easier as you do more of it.

Once you have your shots, bring them into the computer. With a digital camera, this is a relatively straightforward step, as all the images should be identical in size. With film you need to be careful that you scan each image the same: same crop, same resolution, same size, everything the same. That will help you line up the images better in the software.

Stitching Programs

There are two basic ways of dealing with a panoramic image shot with multiple exposures. You can use a stitching program that does the work for you, or you can use image-processing software that has layers and you do it yourself. There are advantages and disadvantages to each method. Stitching programs (such as ArcSoft's Panorama Maker, www.arcsoft.com, or the Photomerge option in both Photoshop and Photoshop Elements, www.adobe.com) are very easy, but need distinct objects in the overlapped areas in order to work best. In addition, they should have a healthy overlap (30-50%) to do their stitching of images. They usually have some "morphing" capabilities that allow the images to blend better where things don't match perfectly.

With a stitching program, the steps are pretty straightforward. First, you need to check all of your photos to be sure they are consistent in size and tonality. Any big changes in brightness, for example, will show up as unevenness in the final image. Make any adjustments needed to give them the required consistency, before you try to stitch them

▲ These two photos were shot with the deliberate 30% overlap, so they could be more easily stitched together in a panoramic shot.

▶ ArcSoft's Panorama Maker is an inexpensive, semi-automated way to create panoramic prints.

together and then import them into your stitching program. While some programs claim to be able to figure out the order of your photos automatically, you can usually help the program work more efficiently, if you put the pictures in order from left to right (or top to bottom).

Then you tell the program to go to work. Depending on the processing speed and RAM of your computer, this will take a little time. RAM is really critical as panoramic photos can get quite large. Once the processing is complete, take a look at your photo. You may find a section giving you a problem with uneven tones. You may have to go back and adjust that photo, then redo the panoramic. Minor problems can often be corrected with the cloning tool. You'll usually have to do a crop to the final image to fix the edges.

EPSON COMPLETE GUIDE TO DIGITAL PRINTING

▲ A strong graphic element in the overlap area of photos that are used for a panoramic image will help you put them together.

◀ With imaging programs that offer layers, you can carefully control how your panoramic shots come together.

Layered Panoramics

Using layers to build a panoramic does take more work, but they can be more effective when you have less overlap, the overlap is not distinct or you have movement between shots. In the last case, you need to make some decisions as to what to keep and what to leave out in the overlapped areas that the automated stitching programs won't make.

Layered panoramics can give you more precision in matching pieces of the image, too. You'll have the easiest time if your program includes both layers and layer masks, such as Adobe Photoshop. These added layers do increase the demands on your system, so need to be sure you have enough RAM. Most photographers find that 512 MB is a comfortable minimum unless you are making really big pans. The steps are as follows:

1 Bring your images into the software. Here is where a digital camera really shines, because, as long as you were careful in how you set up the camera, the photos will line up as expected.

2 Create a blank page that is slightly larger than your photos' depth and as long as the total number of photos times their width. For example, suppose you have a 5 x 7 inch size for a single image and three total images for the panorama. The blank page should then be about six inches deep (this covers the five inch side) and 21 inches long (to include all three photos lined up). You won't actually need the full width, because the photos overlap, but it helps to have the working space when you are beginning.

▲**The final shot now ready for printing.**

3 Drag or copy and paste the photos on to the blank page. Each will go on separate layers.

4 Starting with the left photo from the pan series, move it to the far left of the working layered panoramic and make it the bottom layer. Then move the next image to the left until it overlaps the first in approximately the right alignment.

5 Make your overlapping layer somewhat transparent and move it around until it lines up with the first layer as best as you can. It might not be perfect, but that's okay. Now, make it opaque again.

6 Blend the edge of the two layers together by removing parts of the top image, letting the good parts of the lower image show through. If your program includes it, a layer mask is the best way to gain control over the removal

process, including being able to bring back things that you took out by mistake. Try using soft brushes in your layer mask. Soft eraser tools on programs without a layer mask can help, too, although they often require a lot of "doing and undoing" to get it right. Work until the two photos look as one. You may need to do some minor corrections with the clone tool.

7 Repeat the process for each individual image of the panoramic series.

8 Fix the edges. It is rare that all of the individual shots will line up exactly. Use your crop tool to trim the edges and complete the panoramic.

9 You can then do your normal finishing touches to an image, such as flattening and sharpening the image with your standard Unsharp Mask settings.

Panoramic Skies

The sky part of a constructed panoramic photo is one place where you will often run into problems. This is one area where inconsistencies of tone can really make an otherwise good photo look bad.

Probably the easiest way to fix skies is to use a combination of selections and layers. Let's look at how you would do this to replace an entire sky. This is easiest to do with a small sky area without clouds (which will show problems more, anyway).

1 Select the sky

Use the Magic Wand selection tool or other automatic edge selection tools. Select the whole sky, even if you have to do it in stages, adding in parts from different layers. You may need to add a very slight feather (just a few pixels) to blend the edge

2 Choose sky colors

Pick up colors from the original sky. In Photoshop and Photoshop Elements, you can select a foreground and a background color. Double click on the color icon and you will get the Color Picker. Move your cursor over the pan sky and it will turn to an Eyedropper. If there is any color in the sky at all, click on a dark color for the foreground and a light color for the background, since most skies blend from dark to light as they get close to the horizon. Otherwise pick good sky colors from the Color Picker palette.

3 Fill the selection with the sky colors

Using the Gradient tool, create a gradient of your sky colors from dark to light through your selected sky area, keeping the dark at the top and the light at the bottom. Experiment with your positioning of the start and stop points of your gradient line. You work a gradient by clicking once to start the gradient, then, keeping the mouse button depressed, you move to a new spot where the gradient will end and release. The gradient will blend over that distance.

4 Adjust the new sky color and tone

Use the Hue/Saturation and Brightness/Contrast controls to make the sky look natural.

5 Use layers for more control

If you make this new sky on a new layer, you gain a lot more control. You will be able to blend the edges easier as well as adjust its color and strength without affecting anything else. You may also find that experimenting with Layer Modes will help.

6 Add noise to the sky

The new colors are smooth and don't look very photographic. Enlarge a section of the photo so you can see the grain in the non-sky part of the photo and add some noise to the sky colors (in the Filters menu) to match. Usually, you set the grain very low and you may even need to add a slight Gaussian blur to it to make it match the rest of the photo.

Printing the Panoramic

Once you complete your panoramic image, you'll want to print it out on your Epson printer. This is not a problem except that you need to have long paper. You can buy Epson photo-quality paper in rolls that can be either used with a roll feeder or cut to be single-sheet fed into the printer. You can also buy sheets of paper precut to a standard panoramic size of 8.3 x 23.4 inches.

When you print, you do need to tell your printer what kind of paper it is and the size. Obviously, a very big panoramic will take some time to print. Be careful to support the paper carefully both going into the printer and coming out so it does not fold or crease and damage your photo.

© Joseph R. Meehan

© Joseph R. Meehan

© Joseph R. Meehan

© Joseph R. Meehan

© Joseph R. Meehan

Photographer

Joseph R. Meehan

Panoramics and More

Joe Meehan's specialty is large panoramic photography. He is also a well-known photography book author who speaks at seminars across the country and is technical editor of *Photo District News*. "All the Epson photo printers are a blessing because they will print panoramic prints," he says. "In the 6 x 17, 1:3 aspect ratio format, for example, this means being able to make a stunning color print measuring roughly 1 x 3 feet in size, from a machine costing less than a good SLR."

He started using Epson printers when the first photo model was introduced. "Back in those days, there were no ink jet photo-type papers available, so I would process unexposed black-and-white resin-coated conventional print paper in my darkroom, and then use it in the Epson to get a photo print look."

Today, Meehan has a wall of Epson printers for a whole variety of purposes, from print sales to illustrations for his seminars on digital print output. He uses prints as final art for the books he writes on photographic methods. His favorite papers include Epson's Premium Luster, ColorLife, and Heavyweight Matte paper.

Years ago, he would spend hours in a darkroom or farm out volume printing to a lab. Now, virtually all of his color prints are made on Epson printers, which often run continuously while he does other things in his office.

"Doing your own printing opens up all sorts of chances to experiment, which is why I always maintained a darkroom in my commercial business. But the ease with which I can now print out four or six variations of the same image on an 11 x 17 sheet of ink jet paper in a matter of a few minutes surpasses anything I was able to do previously in my darkroom. This ability has really expanded the whole creative process for me."

He has also started to present clients with variations, which he says they really appreciate. Meehan says that the ink jet printer has now given him complete control over the whole creative process with a level of speed, convenience and range of variations that he has never experienced before.

"The handwriting is really on the wall," Meehan says. "Digital printing is gaining in acceptance among photographers, art buyers, and publishers. In fact, it is now considered to be a form of high-quality print making. In addition, the ability to use different papers and ink sets offers more opportunities to achieve a personal interpretation than any other form of printing."

Meehan's Web site is www.josephmeehan.com.

Long-Lived Prints

When ink jets first came out with photo-quality printing, they had a real limitation, as the dyes used for the colors faded. With some of the earliest photo-quality printers, this life was as short as six months. Ink jet printers rivaled traditional prints in color and tone, but not in longevity.

The life of a print was a serious issue for photographers. They wanted to be able to display photos for longer than a few months, and they wanted to give away, or sell, prints that could be enjoyed for years.

Epson was the first manufacturer to address this concern of photographers. The company came out with dye-based inks that would last as long as traditional photo prints when used with the appropriate papers. This was a major breakthrough.

Next, Epson came out with pigment-based inks that actually would work in an ink jet printer and not clog the heads (a problem with that type of ink). These inks could last over 100 years. Although they weren't quite up to the colors of dye-based inks, they were really quite good. Of course, Epson has gone beyond that now, offering both dye-based and pigmented inks with brilliant color and very long life.

Archival Qualities

Loosely defined, archival refers to print longevity. To be considered archival, a print must look its best without noticeable fading or color shifts for a significant amount of time. Controversy occurs over exactly how long this time period must be and what is noticeable fading or color change. Light has the greatest influence on print life, but storage conditions, storage materials, heat, and humidity also have an effect.

Testing today is done by exposing prints to high-intensity light, which simulates light exposure over many years. Henry Wilhelm is considered by many to be the expert in archival research. His website (www.wilhelm-research.com) has important information about how different inks and papers last over time. Unfortunately, some independent manufacturers have made archival claims based on lower testing standards than Wilhelm's. If print longevity is important, check his latest information.

It is important to understand that archival print qualities are not about just ink or paper. There are three factors that work together to affect print life: ink, paper, and storage

Ink and Paper

Epson uses two basic types of inks: dye-based and pigmented. Printers using Epson pigment-based Ultrachrome and DuraBrite inks resist fading longer than any dye-based inks. However, with the right paper, dye-based inks will retain their colors for a long time. The latter do provide some advantages in printing speed and the highest color gamut or range.

With Epson's dye-based photo inks, you can expect a print to resist fading (Lightfast rating) for over 20 years when Epson Matte Paper Heavyweight is used and seven years with standard Epson Photo Paper. These are well within the range of life of traditional color prints from the local minilab.

Life of typical displayed and framed Epson prints, based on independent testing from Wilhelm Research Labs (www.Wilhelm-research.com):

Epson Photo Paper Type	Dye-based Inks	DuraBrite Pigment Inks	Ultrachrome Pigment Inks
Premium Glossy	5 years	28 years	50 years
Premium Luster	6 years	27 years	47 years
Matte Paper Heavyweight	18 years	72 years	. . .
Archival/Enhanced Matte Paper	. . .	54 years	62 years
Radiant White Watercolor Paper	. . .	. . .	90 years

◀ Choosing the right paper will affect the life of your print.

Archival storage is essential for long-lived prints. These metal-edged boxes from archivalmethods.com feature a removable top with hinged, drop-front panel on the long side. This opens the box so that dog-earing is minimized. ▶

When Epson's UltraChrome inks are used with Epson matte-type papers or Epson Premium Photo Papers, expect them to last decades without fading. Epson's DuraBrite Ink is a pigment-based ink used with certain Epson four-color printers and has similar qualities, but is not used with photo printers.

The ratings here are based on accelerated testing of prints displayed indoors, under glass, under fluorescent lights. Severe conditions, such as prints under direct sunlight, may cause shorter lives.

Image Storage

The better the conditions a print is stored in, the longer its life will be. Typically, dye-based prints can stand handling better than pigmented inks, because they are absorbed into the paper. While quite durable, pigmented ink surfaces are more easily scratched and damaged than dye-based prints.

If a print is kept out of the light, in a protected album or other storage container, you can expect a very long life indeed. The album or storage container, however, should be made of archival materials (such as acid-free paper), so that it doesn't interact with the prints.

On display, a print should be framed and kept behind glass for longest life. Be sure the framing materials, such as the matte and mounting boards, are archival quality, or acid-free. And remember that display in bright sunlight or near fluorescents will shorten a print's life.

◀ **Properly stored, Epson ink jet prints can last a very long time.**

◀ **A faded photo is never fun. Use the right printer and papers, frame your photos and store them well to ensure their longevity.**

© Greg Gorman

© Greg Gorman

© Greg Gorman

Greg Gorman

Celebrity Personalities

Greg Gorman is one of the most sought after and respected photographers in the industry. From personality portraits and advertising campaigns to magazine layouts and fine art work, Gorman has developed and showcased a discriminating and unique style in his imaging. One of his strengths has been photographing noted motion picture and music personalities, as well as icons from the sports world. His work has been used for feature film advertising and publicity campaigns as well as album covers. In addition to gallery exhibitions, Gorman's work has been exhibited in museum shows in North America and Europe and is consistently featured in publications throughout the world.

In 1968, knowing little about photography, Gorman borrowed a friend's camera to take some pictures at a Jimi Hendrix concert. When he saw the images coming up in the developer tray, he was hooked on photography. Gorman says he still gets excited every time he takes a picture. Over the past few years, what has really captured his attention is the digital revolution.

Gorman uses both desktop and large format Epson ink jet printers to print his images, and he says they have changed his career. The digital revolution has allowed Gorman to go back into the darkroom, which is something he hadn't done in 30 years. Except this time it's a digital darkroom. He has found that working digitally is quicker, more efficient, and more effective than the traditional analog process.

"I get incredible quality with my Epson printers, and I'm in complete control," Gorman says. "I can see my vision from the concept to the finished product, whereas before I was relying on lab technicians to try to give me what they thought I wanted. Now I have complete control. Nothing is more satisfying than seeing my image come off the printer the way I perceived it."

In addition to the right printers, the right ink and paper are critical for Gorman's work. He looks for high contrast, deep, saturated colors, strong blacks, and good shadow detail, and he needs images that will last. He says Epson's seven-color UltraChrome inks, which are pigment-based, give him the strong blacks he wants in his prints, along with permanence.

"I want my prints to be around long after I'm gone. With Epson printers I get images that not only will look great but also will last for generations."

EPSON COMPLETE GUIDE TO DIGITAL PRINTING

Caring for your Printer

Your Epson printer will provide excellent service to you for many, many prints. But like all mechanical and digital devices, wear and tear, as well as computer conflicts, can cause problems.

The life of a printer depends on your printing needs. There is no question the expensive graphic arts ink jets, which often have similar printing specifications to much lower priced units, will print a volume of prints every day without failure much longer than a value-priced printer. You do get what you pay for. However, if you only print a few photos per week, you probably don't need a high-priced printer designed for the graphic artist, or wedding photographer, who cranks out lots of photos.

In addition, you may want to upgrade your printer, if new technology offers something valuable to you. Seven-color printers, for example, are a real boon for black-and-white printing. So, if you want to do a lot of that type of printing and only have a four- or six-color printer, it may be an excellent investment.

Regardless of your printer, there are some things you can do to keep your Epson printer working at its best. Your printer's manual will cover much of this in more detail specific to your unit than I can do in the book, but I will give you some hints on maintaining your printer.

On and Off

This seems like such a basic thing. How can turning a printer on and off be a problem? It isn't unless you turn it on and off from a power strip. Never do that. When you turn a printer off, it parks the heads in a very specific place. If you turn the printer off at a power strip, it may or may not be parked properly. This can lead to the head drying out and clogging.

If you are using the printer on a daily basis, you can just leave it on. You should turn the printer off if it is not going to be used for a few days. This allows it to park its heads, which maintains them properly. However, your printer does work best when used regularly, so turn on your printer and make a small print at least every couple of weeks (if not more often) to keep it functioning well.

▲ **Know your printer's controls and always turn it on and off with the power button.**

Print Head Cleaning

A common ink jet printing problem is a clogged head. Typically, you'll see either streaks of ink or else lines of white where ink did not print. If you don't use your Epson printer regularly, the inks dry in the tips of the nozzles and clog the heads. When to clean depends on environmental conditions, but a quick cleaning never hurts at any time.

On Epson printers, you can initiate cleaning in two ways: on the printer or through software. There is a cleaning button on the front of the printer (check your manual for exact placement). Hold it down for three seconds and the unit will start a cleaning cycle.

For heavy-duty cleaning of a serious clog, it is best to use the head-cleaning utility in the software. You get to it through the printer driver. You can right-click the printer icon in the Windows taskbar (or get to it through the Start menu, Settings, and Printers) and select Head Cleaning. On a Mac, open the File menu and choose Page Setup or Print. Then, click the Utility and Head-Cleaning buttons in that order. Follow the on-screen instructions, then use the Nozzle Check command to be sure the head is clean. Multiple cleaning passes will help, especially if the printer has been sitting for many weeks.

▲ **A clogged printer head (left photo) quickly degrades image quality.**

▲ **All Epson printer drivers have a utility section for printer maintenance.**

◀ **In this detail, you can see how a clogged head printed blacks poorly (left image).**

Whichever technique you use, the printer will make a bit of noise while it works. This is normal. The green power light will flash while it is working. Be sure that you do not turn the printer off while it is cleaning its heads.

Once done, you should use the head-cleaning utility to check the nozzles on the head. Click on Print nozzle check pattern, then Print. Check your page when it comes out. If the printed pattern is nice and solid with no gaps or lines, the head is clean. If it is streaky, try cleaning again.

If you do this a few times and you still see streaking, you can try turning the printer off and letting it sit overnight. According to Epson, this allows dried ink to soften. Then try cleaning again. You may also find that the old ink cartridge just isn't helping. You can install a new one and the heads may clean better.

Clogged heads can come from using non-Epson ink cartridges. Epson wants its customers to have success with their prints, so they have a very high standard of ink quality. Not all independent cartridges will meet those standards. This can be a big problem because the head is built into the printer and cannot be easily cleaned if clogged by bad ink. So, to minimize clog problems, use Epson ink.

Aligning the Print Head

You may never have to align your printer's head. This is not a preventative maintenance procedure. You only need to align the head if your prints show vertical lines that don't connect.

Print head alignment is done through the Epson printer software, so the ink jet must be connected to the computer. Open the printer utilities as described above, but instead of choosing head cleaning, you will choose the Print Head Alignment button. From here, you follow the instructions on the screen. You will be making a test print then choosing lines that look most precisely aligned. I find that this is best done quickly. If you agonize over the choices, it can be really hard to see the differences.

Cleaning the Printer

A printer gets dusty over time. To keep it at its peak, clean it a few times a year. This is a pretty simple thing to do, but be sure you disconnect both the power plug and the computer cable before starting.

Use a soft brush to clean dust and dirt from the sheet feeder. You can use the same brush inside the printer, but avoid the gears. A can of compressed air can be used to get rid of dust and debris, but never shake it or get the nozzle too close to moving parts. Clean ink out of the inside of the printer with a soft, slightly damp (not wet) cloth. Use a soft, slightly damp cloth on the outside as well.

Never use any solvents or oils, especially cleaners with alcohol, as this can damage the plastic. Don't use the cleaning sheets that sometimes come with printing papers as these can actually cause problems, including jamming inside the printer.

Troubleshooting—Common Printer Problems

1
Driver problems

It is possible to have your driver fail to work properly in any number of ways. Removing it and re-installing the driver can help. In addition, it is always a good idea to check Epson's Web site every once in a while to see if a new, improved driver or software patches have been posted.

2
White lines or missing colors

These are classic signs of a clogged print head (although missing colors may be a sign of a low ink cartridge). Clean the head, use multiple passes if necessary, and check the nozzle print pattern (see your manual).

3
Banding or splotchy colors

Be sure you have the right paper and driver setting. Some non-Epson papers can print very poorly in this way. In addition, some papers have a "right" side and a "wrong" side. If you print on the "wrong" side, you will get some quite odd ink patterns on the photo. If the paper and driver setting is right, try cleaning the print head as mentioned above, or you may need a new ink cartridge.

4
Faint or low contrast prints

This can come from a number of sources, including clogged ink heads. However, most often, this problem is caused by the use of the wrong printer driver setting and the wrong paper. This can also be caused by old ink cartridges or old paper.

5
Printing seems slow

Check your image size. Big, high-resolution images require RAM and hard-drive space to print. Be sure you have enough of each. You may need to add both, but RAM is especially important.

6
Run a printer check

It can be useful to know if the printer or the computer is the source of any problem. Turn off the printer and computer, and then disconnect the printer. Hold down the maintenance button (check your manual) and at the same time push and release the power button. Keep holding the maintenance button until the green power light flashes.
The printer will print a test page. If it prints okay, then the problem is most likely in the computer or in the cable connection.

7
Prints look grainy

This is usually a function of the image, so check to see that you aren't seeing real grain or digital noise (see Grain and Noise Management in Chapter 8 for more information). This can also be an issue of trying to make a print from a file that has a low image resolution.

8
Check the manual

I know...the joke is that no one ever reads the manual. Yet, Epson manuals have excellent troubleshooting guides that go far beyond the scope of this chapter, plus it is specifically for your printer.

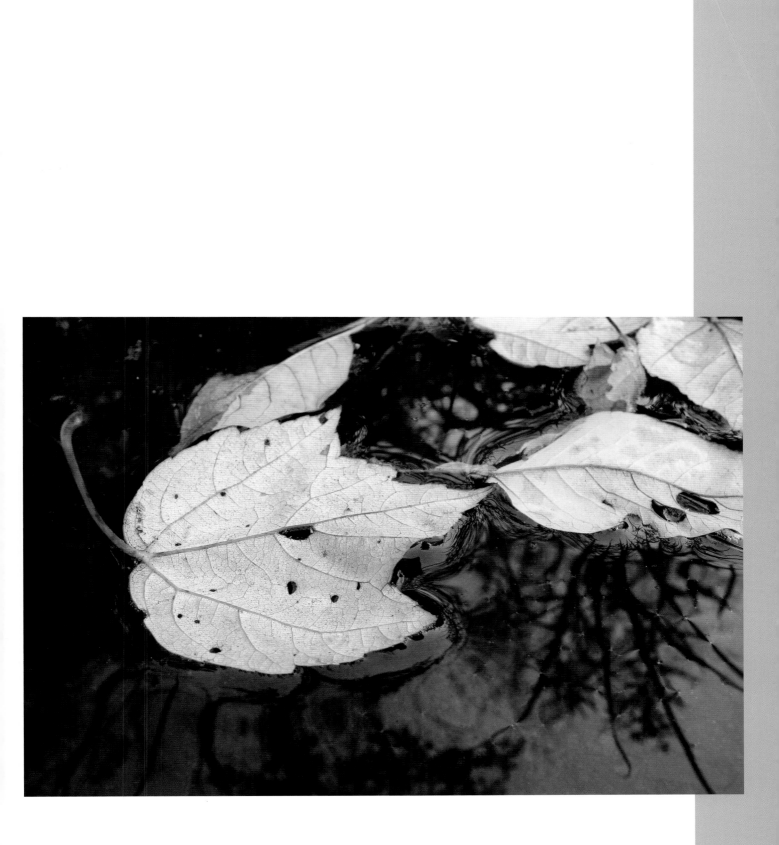

Index

Notes